LEON
HAPPY
CURRIES

BY REBECCA SEAL & JOHN VINCENT

conran
OCTOPUS

CONTENTS

INTRODUCTION........................4

MILD 12

FIERY 36

CREAMY 58

SPEEDY......................86

SLOW.........................126

SIDES.........................152

BREAD.........................196

PICKLES & CHUTNEYS 212

INDEX......................218

ABOUT THE AUTHORS 222

ACKNOWLEDGMENTS 223

KEY

WF
WHEAT FREE

GF
GLUTEN FREE

DF
DAIRY FREE

V
VEGETARIAN

Ve
VEGAN

NF
NUT FREE

SoF
SOY FREE

SUITABLE FOR FREEZING

INTRODUCTION

Did you know that in India there is no such thing as curry? Curry, seemingly that most Asian of all foods, was a word invented by Portuguese and British colonialists surrounded by exotic Indian foods in the fifteenth and sixteenth centuries. They used it to describe the unfamiliar food they encountered on their travels.

As a word its roots are uncertain, but at LEON we are fairly sure that it came from the Tamil "kari," meaning "grilled" or "to bite and chew" or even just a kind of sauce (or possibly from a very old English word for *stew*). These various definitions have as much specificity as the modern "curry," which, in English, describes everything from a rich, fragrant coconut-based soup to a bowl of spice-rubbed grilled meat—and everything in between. But in India, and across much of Asia, dishes we think of as curry are called by their own particular names.

Soon the idea of curry spread across the British and Portuguese Empires via sailors, traders and the Indian cooks who traveled with them. Bold flavors and spices were diluted to suit meeker British palates until *Mrs Beeton's Book of Household Management* recorded a recipe in 1861 that listed apples, cream and meat as the main ingredients (with just a dash of curry powder).

During the following centuries, as trade routes and whole communities of people crossed back and forth, the idea of curry spread even further—to the Caribbean, to southern Africa, to the islands of the Indian Ocean and the South Pacific, and adopted the sumptuous dishes of these countries too.

In this way, curry has become a magical world of exotic flavors and spice—and, at LEON, those are some of our favorite things. Curry can be so deliciously varied—fresh, light, healthy, sour, hot, creamy, mild, soothing or rich, and we wanted to create a collection of the very best we've tasted. We've found joy in our journey through spice and time, collecting recipes from friends, the LEON team, family, local restaurants and our travel diaries.

So really, curry can mean anything you want it to. We think that curry is many delicious, happy things. We hope you think so too.

Rebecca and John

THE WELL-STOCKED KITCHEN

SPICES

asafetida

black mustard seeds

black peppercorns

black salt

green cardamom pods

cayenne pepper

chaat masala

dried chili peppers

crushed red pepper

chili powder

cinnamon (whole sticks & ground)

cloves (whole)

coriander (seeds & ground)

cumin (seeds & ground)

curry powder (Caribbean & Madras)

fennel seeds

fenugreek seeds

dried fenugreek leaves (methi)

garam masala

ground mace

ground turmeric

mustard seeds

nigella seeds

whole nutmeg

paprika (sweet & smoked)

saffron

FREEZER

sustainable seafood

MSC-certified salmon fillets

lime leaves

fresh curry leaves

peas

fenugreek leaves (methi)

whole leaf spinach

ready-made paratha

ready-made naan

ready-made rotis/ chapatis

FRIDGE

high-welfare meat (ideally organic)

sustainably sourced fish

fish sauce

galangal paste

tamarind paste

ghee (can be vegan)

whole-milk plain yogurt (can be nondairy)

paneer

good-quality Thai curry pastes

nam prik pao (Thai chili paste)

extra-firm tofu (non-GMO/organic)

FRESH

lemons and limes
cauliflower
onions
scallions
shallots
ginger
garlic
lemon grass
hot & mild peppers
Thai basil
cilantro
mint
bay leaves
thyme
kale
sweet potatoes
green beans
organic/free-range eggs

CUPBOARD

canned tomatoes
tomato purée
canned garbanzo beans
canned kala chana (black chickpeas)
canned kidney beans
canned black beans
coconut milk
desiccated coconut
sticky rice
basmati rice
mixed wild & basmati rice
black rice
jasmine rice
split peas
red lentils
split white urid dal/lentils

black urid dal/lentils
split yellow mung/moong dal/lentils
extra-firm tofu
noodles
chapati flour (atta)
unroasted cashew nuts
unroasted peanuts
neutral cooking oil (ideally rapeseed)
garbanzo bean/gram flour (besan)
apple cider vinegar
canned unripe green jackfruit

CHOP CHOP

TIPS FOR SPEEDY CURRIES

- Get everything ready before you start—no rummaging around for cumin seeds while garlic burns in the pan.

- Keep your knives sharp for quicker prep.

- Set a bowl next to your cutting board, for the trimmings and scraps.

- Soak rice before it goes in the pan, to speed up its cooking time.

- Bags of frozen ready-made finely chopped onion from the supermarket are your friend.

- Instead of fresh, both ready-made frozen chopped garlic and ginger are great. You can also use ginger paste or garlic paste from a jar if you want, but we reckon they're best used in curries that get a good long cooking, as they don't taste quite right in the quick-cooking dishes.

- It's expensive, but (in a pinch) microwaveable rice is a major time-saver.

LEAVE IT TO THE PROS...

When we sat down to plan this book, we talked about including recipes for authentic homemade pappadam, prawn crackers and all sorts of other delicious things that we love to eat with curries. We do believe in the power of freshly homemade goodies ... most of the time. But we also have busy families and full-time jobs (rather more than full-time, in John's case, running LEON!), so we are always on the lookout for shortcuts—as long as they still taste great.

We have included a recipe for samosas, as well as some for breads, pickles and chutneys, so do try them out, when you have the time (and we're in awe of you if you do). However, if you're passing a specialty shop, or even a big supermarket, you can easily stock up on fresh and frozen flatbreads, such as parathas and naan, and pastries, such as samosas (look for frozen vegetable gyoza dumplings and vegetable spring rolls, too).

Frying your own pappadam or prawn crackers is easy and they are even more delicious than they are ready-made. Buy boxes of uncooked pappadam discs, or translucent uncooked prawn crackers, and cook for just a few seconds each in hot oil.

BASIC STEAMED WHITE RICE

SERVES 4
PREP TIME: UP TO 20 MINS SOAKING • COOK TIME: 12 MINS + STANDING TIME
WF • GF • DF • V • VE • NF • SF

8½ ounces **long-grain rice** (basmati or
    jasmine)
water
salt

*You'll turn to this recipe time and time again as the perfect
accompaniment for countless curries. People often think rice
is difficult to get right but this method will make it perfect every time.*

*It really is worth washing the rice—it removes some of the starch on the
outside of each grain, meaning you get nice, fluffy rice, rather than mushy,
sticky rice. Don't cook it in masses of water either—less is more here.*

== **TIP** ==

As a general rule, allow 2 ounces uncooked
rice per person and adjust recipe
quantities accordingly.

We usually add water by eye, but if you prefer to measure, the best ratio we have
found is 2:1 by volume of water to rice—measure the rice onto your scale using a
mug, keeping count of the number you fill, and then use the mug to measure double
the amount of water for cooking.

Rinse the rice in several changes of cold water. If you're cooking basmati rice, then
it will shorten the cooking time and improve the texture if you can soak the rice
in cold water for 10–30 minutes, but it's not essential if you're pressed for time (or
extremely hungry).

Drain the rice and place in a large saucepan with a tight-fitting lid. If you already
measured the water, add it now, or alternatively add cold water to the pan until it's
about ¾ inch above the rice.

Add a pinch of salt, then set the pan over a medium heat. Bring to a boil, then
cover with a lid and turn the heat down to a simmer. Cook for 12 minutes, then
remove from the heat and remove the lid. Check the texture—it should be almost
completely cooked, but if it's unsoaked basmati, then it might need a dash more
water and 2 more minutes. If it's ready, fluff up the rice with a fork, then cover again
and leave to steam until you are ready to serve.

SPICE IT UP

SPICE BLENDS

We recommend roasting and grinding or blending spices wherever possible, but sometimes there just isn't time. And some recipes, like Japanese curry, are almost always made with a ready-made blend. We keep a stash of mild Madras curry powder and a subtly—but importantly—different tub of Caribbean curry powder, as well as garam masala. For each, it's worth seeking out a really good brand from a specialty shop or online.

HOW TO LOOK AFTER SPICES

Although no spice lasts indefinitely, keeping them in a cool, dark cupboard, and in airtight containers, will lengthen their lives. (Leaving them in open bags lets the flavors escape and mingle; you'll end up with a gently scented cupboard and everything tasting of cumin.) Although supermarkets now stock an impressive range of blends and individual spices, we often buy ours in Asian grocers, where you can get big bags of quality spices for a fraction of the cost. Wherever you buy them, choose packs from the gloomy back of the shelf, where the light won't have done any damage. Whole spices keep longer than powders—and taste better when freshly ground (even better when toasted and freshly ground).

CHILIES

In the UK, the medium-sized chilies we buy in supermarkets can be very mild at certain times of the year. Look out for smaller, hotter chilies, such as bird's-eye or finger chilies. It's not always the case, but little chilies are very often more fiery, with the exception of large frilly-looking Scotch bonnets, which are mouth-numbingly sour and hot. Older, riper chilies tend to be hotter, so if you leave them in the fridge for a while, your mild-mannered supermarket chilies may turn feisty. Green chilies have a more bitter, vegetal flavor, while red ones tend to be sweeter, and sometimes hotter too.

Always taste a little piece of a chili before adding it to a dish (except for the searingly hot beasts, like Scotch bonnets)—once you've added it, you can't take the heat out, but you can always add more later, if you like. When deseeding a chili, to make it milder, remember to remove the white pith, too, as that's actually where the worst of the heat is hiding.

HEALTH

Spices have been used in traditional medicine all over the world for millennia, and gradually more formal research is being done to discover their powers. Turmeric and ginger are thought to be anti-inflammatory (turmeric may be antiviral, antibacterial and antifungal, too); cinnamon is considered an antioxidant and may promote heart health; cayenne and chilies may kick-start the metabolism; fenugreek may help to regulate blood sugar; and, in some alternative medicine practices, cardamom is used to remove toxins from the body.

VEG IT UP

We want our books to be friendly to anyone who chooses to eat fewer or no animal products. In many of our recipes, you can swap the meat, fish or dairy for vegetables, pulses, tofu, or a ready-made meat replacement.

Canned unripe green jackfruit, rinsed, shredded, and with the tougher core removed, is a startlingly good substitute for chicken. So is light seitan, a wheat-based meat replacement that has been used for centuries in Chinese cooking (if you've ever tried mock duck, you've eaten seitan). Dark seitan has a beefier flavor, so can be used instead of red meat. Both are best sliced and browned first, then added to a curry when it's almost ready to serve.

Firm tofu works well instead of salmon or cod in fish curries—just submerge it in the broth in the same way as you would fish, or chop and fry it first to lightly brown. Although we love soft, silky tofu, we tend not to use it in curries, as it can too easily fall apart.

Vegetarians can swap paneer, an Indian cheese, into most meat curries—treat it as we do on page 60, then add towards the end of cooking.

Crunchy vegetables, such as cauliflower, carrots and peppers, work well in many curries, as do sweet potatoes, eggplant, and mushrooms—whether to cook them first depends on how long the curry needs to cook. You can extend meat dishes like keema (see page 145) by adding cooked pulses, such as French or black lentils, or use canned garbanzo or black beans in saucier curries.

Crisp green vegetables, when in season, are excellent in soupy curries—go for long thin spears of broccoli, green beans, sugar snap peas, asparagus, sliced kale, cabbage or slices of zucchini.

CURRY UDON NOODLES

SERVES 2

PREP TIME: 15 MINS • COOK TIME: 30 MINS

NF

2 **eggs**

9 ounces **extra-firm tofu**, cut into
½-inch x 1-inch fingers

2 teaspoons **neutral cooking oil**

1 small **onion**, halved and finely sliced

5 ounces **shiitake mushrooms**, sliced

2 tablespoons **butter**

2 heaped tablespoons **all-purpose flour**

1 tablespoon **mild Indian curry powder**

1 teaspoon **garam masala**

2½ cups hot **dashi stock** (or mix 1
teaspoon **soy sauce**, 1 teaspoon **fish
sauce**, and 2 **vegetable bouillon cubes**
with 2½ cups **hot water**)

5 ounces **dried udon noodles**

soy sauce, to taste

2 **scallions**, finely sliced on a diagonal

1–2 generous pinches of **shichimi
togarashi seasoning**, to garnish
(optional) (to make your own, combine
1 pinch each of some or all of the
following: **sesame seeds**, **black pepper**,
Szechuan pepper, **ground ginger**,
seaweed flakes or **powder**, **crushed
red pepper**, **garlic powder**)

salt, to taste

This curry made its way to Japan from India via the British, which is why it is made with curry powder. It's a gentle, soothing curry, with thick noodles and a Japanese sesame-and-spice seasoning, shichimi togarashi.

Place the eggs in a steamer basket set over a saucepan of simmering water. Steam for 8 minutes, for soft-yolked, hard-boiled eggs. Cool under running cold water, then set aside.

Press the tofu between two sheets of paper towel to squeeze out the moisture. Set a wide deep saucepan over a medium heat and add the oil. When hot, add the tofu and cook until golden and no longer sticking to the pan. Turn each piece and cook until golden again. Remove from the pan and set aside. Add the onions and mushrooms to the pan and sauté for about 5 minutes, until the onion is beginning to soften.

Turn the heat to low and add the butter. When melted, add the flour and cook, stirring, for 3–4 minutes, until combined into a smooth golden roux. Mix in the curry powder and garam masala and cook for a further 2 minutes.

Next, add a little of the hot stock. Mix until smooth, then gradually add the rest. Bring to a simmer, and cook, stirring, until the broth has thickened slightly.

Add the noodles to the pan and cook according to the package instructions, stirring often so they don't clump together. Meanwhile, peel and halve the eggs.

Taste the broth for salt and umami, and add a pinch of salt or dash of soy sauce, as needed. Divide the curry udon between two bowls, decorate with the halved eggs, and sprinkle with the scallions and shichimi togarashi, if using.

MILD

═ TIP ═

Vegans can leave out the eggs and add vegetables, such as Asian greens and thinly sliced carrots or beans. You can also buy ready-made Japanese curry roux.

1960s CHICKEN TIKKA MASALA

SERVES 4

PREP TIME: 25 MINS • MARINATING TIME: 1–24 HOURS • COOK TIME: 45 MINS

NF • SoF

FOR THE MARINADE:

2 tablespoons **freshly squeezed lemon juice**

2 tablespoons **whole-milk plain yogurt**

¾-inch piece of **ginger**, finely grated

1 clove of **garlic**, crushed

¼ teaspoon **chili powder**

½ teaspoon **sweet smoked paprika**

salt and **freshly ground black pepper**

FOR THE CURRY:

1 tablespoon **neutral cooking oil**

1¾ pounds **boneless, skinless chicken breast**, cut into rough 1-inch chunks

3 **onions**, finely chopped

4 cloves of **garlic**, crushed

1½-inch piece of **ginger**, finely grated

2 teaspoons **tomato paste**

seeds from 4 **green cardamom pods**, ground in a mortar and pestle

1 teaspoon **ground coriander**

2 teaspoons **paprika**

1 teaspoon **sweet smoked paprika**

½ teaspoon **ground cinnamon**

1 teaspoon **ground cumin**

2 teaspoons **garam masala**

Chicken tikka, peshwari naan, pappadams and mango chutney made up the first Indian meal John ever ate, in a tandoori house opposite the Old Bailey in London, aged 14. After growing up on spaghetti bolognaise and shepherd's pie, it was revelatory.

Is tikka masala from Glasgow? Or the Punjab? Or Delhi? Was it invented by a Bangladeshi chef in London in the 1960s? Or did the original recipe involve cream of tomato soup, because a Scottish bus driver sent back a plate of chicken tikka he thought was too dry? There are so many stories—and no one knows for sure—but whatever its history, it is one of the most popular curries in Britain and has been for decades. We'd like to thank Madhur Jaffrey and Felicity Cloake—both their recipes played a part in the creation of this one.

You can use this recipe to make a vegetarian or vegan version of tikka masala. Simply substitute the meat with extra-firm tofu or cauliflower, zucchini, or peppers, and use non-dairy full-fat yoghurt (coconut or soy work well) in place of both the dairy yogurt and cream. Fish eaters can make this with firm fish such as salmon, but cut the marinating time to 15 minutes.

Mix all the marinade ingredients together in a bowl and season well with salt and pepper. Use your hands to work the marinade into the chicken, then cover and refrigerate for 1–24 hours.

¼–½ teaspoon **chili powder**,
    to taste
14 ounces **diced tomatoes**
2½ cups **water**
3–5 tablespoons **light cream**
a big handful of **fresh cilantro leaves**
warm **Naan** (see page 198), to serve
salt and **freshly ground black pepper**

(see page 198)

Heat the oil in a large heavy saucepan over a medium heat, add the onions, and gently sauté until soft and beginning to brown, about 8 minutes. Add the garlic, ginger, and tomato paste and cook for a further 3–4 minutes, stirring often.

Add the ground cardamom seeds, ground coriander, paprika, smoked paprika, cinnamon, cumin, garam masala, chili powder, and diced tomatoes to the pan. Cook, stirring and squashing the tomatoes, for about 10 minutes, until the sauce is really thick. Add the water, a generous pinch of salt, and some freshly ground black pepper and bring to a simmer. Cook for about 15 minutes, until the sauce has reduced—it shouldn't be wet, so continue to reduce if necessary.

Meanwhile, heat the broiler. Remove the chicken from the marinade, but don't scrape it off. You can thread the meat onto skewers or cook it resting on a rack in a baking tray (lined with foil for easier cleaning). Place the meat under the broiler, about 4 inches away from the heat, and cook for about 8 minutes on each side, until just charred on the edges.

While the chicken is cooking, remove the sauce from the heat and add 3 tablespoons of the cream. Taste and add more if wished—it should be creamy, but not overwhelmingly so. Carefully purée the sauce in a blender or food processor until smooth. Work in batches if necessary, as some blenders may explode if overfilled with hot liquid. Transfer the sauce back to the pan and keep warm.

When the chicken is ready, stir it into the sauce and cook for a further 5 minutes. Remove from the heat and stir in half of the cilantro leaves. Serve, sprinkled with the remaining cilantro, with naan breads (and three or four other indulgent curries...).

═ TIP ═

You can also barbecue the chicken. Wait until the coals are white, with no flames, and cook the meat at least 8 inches above the coals, so that the chicken cooks through before the marinade burns.

TIP

To make your own Vietnamese curry powder, place the following ingredients in a mortar and pestle or spice grinder and grind to a powder: 5 cloves, ½ teaspoon fennel seeds, ½ teaspoon coriander seeds, 1 teaspoon cumin seeds, scant ½ teaspoon chili powder, a generous pinch of ground nutmeg, 1 teaspoon ground turmeric, a pinch of ground mace, and a pinch of ground cinnamon.

"CA RI GA" VIETNAMESE CHICKEN CURRY

SERVES 4
PREP TIME: 25 MINS • COOK TIME: 1 HOUR
WF • GF (check fish sauce ingredients and serve with rice) • DF • NF • SoF

1 tablespoon **neutral cooking oil**

1 **onion**, finely sliced

4–8 (depending on size) skin-on, bone-in **chicken thighs**, cut into 2 or 3 pieces

1 tablespoon **Vietnamese curry powder** (ready-made or see tip)

4 cloves of **garlic**, crushed

2 tablespoons **tomato paste**

7 ounces (1 small) **sweet potato**, peeled and cut into chunks

7 ounces **potatoes**, cut into chunks

5 ounces (1 large) **carrot**, peeled, halved, and cut into ½-inch pieces

1-inch piece of **ginger**, peeled and cut into 3 long pieces

1 **lemongrass** stalk, bruised

1 **bay leaf**

1 tablespoon **fish sauce**, plus extra

a generous pinch of **sugar**

¾ cup **coconut milk**, from the top of an unshaken can

freshly squeezed lemon juice, to taste

4 sprigs **Thai basil**

salt

2 big handfuls of **fresh cilantro leaves**

4 **scallions**, finely chopped

baguettes or **steamed rice**, to serve

This is our version of a classic soupy Vietnamese chicken and root vegetable curry, which is often served with the Vietnamese version of a French baguette, adopted during the French colonial era.

Thanks to food blogger Ginger and Scotch for turning us on to the power of homemade Vietnamese curry powder—our recipe is loosely based on hers. You can buy it ready-made online and in Asian food stores (we like Vianco Bot Cary) or use mild Madras curry powder.

Heat the oil in a large heavy saucepan with a lid over a high heat. Add the onion and chicken thighs and soften the onions while browning the chicken to a light golden brown. Work in batches, if necesssary. Return all the browned meat to the pan and add the curry powder, garlic, and tomato paste and cook, stirring, for about 3 minutes.

Add the vegetables, ginger, lemongrass, bay leaf, fish sauce, sugar, and enough hot water to cover (2½–3½ cups). Cover with a lid and bring to a gentle simmer, then lower the heat and cook for 30 minutes.

Remove the lid, add the coconut milk, and bring back to a simmer. Cook, uncovered, for a further 10 minutes, until the chicken is cooked through and the vegetables are tender. Remove and discard the lemongrass and ginger.

Remove from the heat and add a generous squeeze of lemon and the Thai basil. Stir, then taste and add more fish sauce or salt, or lemon juice, if needed. Divide among wide bowls and sprinkle over the cilantro leaves and scallions.

Serve with hunks of baguette, or steamed rice.

MILD

MASSAMAN CURRY

SERVES 4
PREP TIME: 25 MINS • COOK TIME: 2½ HOURS
WF • GF • DF • SoF • SUITABLE FOR FREEZING

FOR THE PASTE:

½ teaspoon **coriander seeds**

½ teaspoon **cumin seeds**

4 **cloves**

seeds from 5 **green cardamom pods**

¼ teaspoon **ground cinnamon**

½ teaspoon **crushed red pepper**

¼ teaspoon **ground mace**

a pinch of **freshly grated nutmeg**

freshly ground black pepper

1 teaspoon **galangal paste**

1 **shallot**, very finely chopped

1 **lemongrass** stalk, outer layer removed,
    very finely chopped

3 cloves of **garlic**, crushed

1 teaspoon **fish sauce**

FOR THE CURRY:

13.5-ounce can **coconut milk**, unshaken

1½ pounds **chuck steak**, cut into small chunks

12 ounces **potatoes**, cut into small chunks

½ a small **onion**, finely sliced

6 **lime leaves**

fish sauce, to taste

tamarind paste or **concentrate**, to taste

unsalted peanuts or **cashew nuts**,
    to serve

sticky rice, to serve

Rebecca was completely bewildered when she arrived in Bangkok for the first time when she was nineteen—everything seemed extraordinary. But on her first night in a backpackers' hostel, she had this mellow curry for dinner and all was well with the world. Massaman is different to most other Thai curries—there are no fiery chilies. The curry base works with chicken, fish, or veg—just reduce the cooking time accordingly and only add water as needed, rather than the full amount.

For the paste, place all the dry spices and a generous grinding of black pepper in a mortar and pestle and grind to a powder. Add the galangal paste, shallot, lemongrass, and garlic, and pound to a very smooth paste. Stir in the fish sauce.

Spoon a dollop of the thick cream from the top of the coconut milk can into a large heavy saucepan with a lid, set over a medium heat. Let it melt and begin to sizzle, then add the paste (or 3 tablespoons of ready-made curry paste) and fry for 3–4 minutes, until fragrant. When the paste develops an oily sheen, add the remaining coconut milk and ¾ cup hot water and bring gently to a simmer. Add the beef, then partially cover and simmer on the lowest possible heat for 1½–2 hours, or until the beef is tender. Keep an eye on liquid levels—the sauce needs to reduce and thicken a little, but should never become dry or sticky, so add splashes of water when needed.

Add the potatoes and onion, plus a little water if there isn't enough liquid to cover, and bring back to a simmer. Cook for 12–15 minutes, or until the potatoes are tender but not falling apart. Towards the end of cooking, add the lime leaves and 1 teaspoon each of fish sauce and tamarind paste. Taste, adding more of each until you're happy with the balance of sour and salt. Add the nuts and serve with the rice.

≡ TIP ≡

To turn this into
a Korean-style curry
dish, serve some kimchi
(a fermented cabbage
condiment) alongside.

THÉRÈSE'S CHICKEN KATSU AND CURRY SAUCE

SERVES 4

PREP TIME: 25 MINS • COOK TIME: 40 MINS

NF

4 skinless, boneless **chicken thighs**

5 ounces **all-purpose flour**

2 **eggs**, beaten

14 ounces **panko breadcrumbs**

2 tablespoons **cooking oil**

salt and **freshly ground black pepper**

steamed rice, to serve

FOR THE SAUCE:

1½ tablespoons **neutral cooking oil**

1 **onion**, finely chopped

4 ounces (1 medium) **carrot**, finely diced

2 cloves of **garlic**, finely chopped

½ teaspoon **ground cumin**

1 tablespoon **Madras curry powder**

1 teaspoon **ground turmeric**

¾ cup **chicken stock**

1½ tablespoons **soy sauce**

2 teaspoons **honey** (or more, to taste)

1 tablespoon **corn starch** mixed into a
     smooth paste with 2 tablespoons **water**

2 tablespoons **light cream**

1 teaspoon **garam masala**

salt and **freshly ground black pepper**

We asked LEON's Instagram followers for their best curry recipes and the winners got the chance to have their recipe in this book. We loved Thérèse Gaughan's take on Japanese chicken katsu. For more of her recipes, check out her website: www.kitchenexile.com.

To make the sauce, heat the oil in a saucepan over a low heat, add the onion, carrot, and garlic and fry for 10–15 minutes, stirring, until softened. Add the cumin, curry powder, and turmeric and cook, stirring often, for 5 minutes. Stir in the stock, soy sauce, and honey and cook for a further 10 minutes. Add the corn starch paste and the cream and cook, stirring, until it starts to thicken (add up to 4 tablespoons of water if it gets too thick). Add the garam masala and season to taste with salt and pepper (add a little more honey, if you prefer it sweet). Keep warm.

Lay the chicken thighs on a cutting board, cover with plastic wrap, and pound with a rolling pin to ½ inch thick. If this makes the pieces very large, cut in half. Place the flour on a plate and season. Place the eggs in a wide bowl and the breadcrumbs on a separate plate. Dip the chicken pieces first into the flour, then the egg, and finally into the breadcrumbs, ensuring they are well coated.

Heat the oil in a skillet over a low heat. When hot, fry the chicken for 7–10 minutes, turning every 3 minutes, until cooked through. Drain on paper towel. (You may need to work in batches. Wipe out the pan and start each batch with fresh oil.)

Slice the katsu chicken into ¾-inch strips, and serve with the sauce and rice.

EVERYDAY DHAL

SERVES 4 WITH LEFTOVERS
PREP TIME: 10 MINS • COOK TIME: 55 MINS
WF • GF • DF • V • Ve • NF • SoF • SUITABLE FOR FREEZING

7 ounces **yellow split peas**, picked over
and rinsed

7 ounces **red split lentils**

3 tablespoons **neutral cooking oil**

1 **onion**, finely chopped

3 cloves of **garlic**, crushed or finely grated

1-inch piece of **ginger**, peeled and
finely grated

2 teaspoons **black mustard seeds**

1 teaspoon **ground turmeric**

1 teaspoon **cumin seeds**

1 teaspoon **ground coriander**

½ teaspoon **garam masala**

1–3 teaspoons finely chopped **red chili
pepper**, to taste

½–1 teaspoon **crushed red pepper**

a squeeze of **lime** or **lemon juice**

salt and **freshly ground black pepper**

a handful of **fresh cilantro**, to garnish

TO SERVE:

Parathas (see pages 205–206)

plain yogurt or **Raita** (see pages 163–164)

spicy chutney or **Lime Pickle** (see page 214)

Dhal is an Indian staple, a lentil-based curry that can be as soupy or as thick as you like. We can't get enough and batch-cook it so we always have a portion (or 10) in the freezer. Eat with flatbreads, pickles and yogurt.

Place the yellow split peas and 4¼ cups of water in a large deep saucepan with a lid and bring to a rolling boil. Use a large spoon to skim off and discard any scum that rises to the surface. Turn the heat down to a simmer, cover, and cook for 30 minutes.

Add the red lentils to the pan along with another 4¼ cups of water, cover, and cook for a further 20 minutes, or until the red lentils are soft and collapsing into the broth.

Meanwhile, make the spice mixture. Add 1 tablespoon of the oil to a skillet set over a medium heat. Add the onion and cook for 12–15 minutes, stirring often, until caramelized and brown. Add the garlic and ginger and cook for 2–3 minutes, then add the remaining oil and the mustard seeds. When they begin to pop, add the rest of the spices, the chili pepper, the crushed red pepper, and a generous pinch of black pepper. Cook until the spices are fragrant but not scorched.

When the split peas are soft and the lentils have collapsed, remove the dhal pan from the heat. Pour in the hot spice mixture, including the oil, and stir. Add some salt, then taste and add more as needed (you can also add more hot water, if you like a soupier dhal). Just before serving, squeeze in a little fresh lemon or lime juice, and stir again.

Serve garnished with a little fresh cilantro and eat hot, with parathas, plain yogurt or raita, and spicy chutney or pickles.

≡ TIP ≡

You can do so much with dhal: add shredded spinach, chopped tomatoes, cauliflower florets, or finely diced potato to the pan, and cook in the dhal. Flavor with curry leaves, bay leaves, or cardamom.

LIPU'S BENGALI FISH TENGA

SERVES 6–8

PREP TIME: 15 MINS • COOK TIME: 35 MINS

WF • GF • DF • NF • SoF

2–3 tablespoons **neutral cooking oil**

1 medium **onion**, finely sliced

a pinch of **salt**

3 cloves of **garlic**, finely sliced

¼ teaspoon **ground turmeric**

14 ounces **canned diced tomatoes** or chopped **fresh tomatoes**

1 pound firm-fleshed **fish**, such as **trout**, **salmon**, **turbot**, or **monkfish** (ideally bone-in) in large pieces

1¾ cups **freshly boiled water**

TO SERVE:

a handful of **fresh cilantro**

2–3 finely sliced **green chili peppers**

plain rice

Lipu is mum to Shumi, a very good friend of LEON: "This is Bengal's answer to France's bouillabaisse. An astringent, soothing broth made with tomatoes and fresh herbs, it is usually eaten at the end of a meal as a palate cleanser. It can be made vegan by swapping out the fish for sliced zucchini or squash, cucumbers or even unripe melon."

Heat 2 tablespoons of the oil in a heavy saucepan with a lid over a medium-low heat. When hot, add the onion and salt and cook until soft and translucent. Add the garlic and continue to cook, until the garlic starts to color a little, then add the ground turmeric and cook until fragrant and the oil separates from the onions.

Add the tomatoes and continue to cook until the tomatoes and onions have completely broken down, adding the final tablespoon of oil if needed. Add the fish and cook for 1–2 minutes, gently stirring to coat it in the onion and spice mixture.

Add the hot water and bring to a simmer without stirring. Cover with a lid, reduce the heat to low, and cook for 5–10 minutes, or until the fish is opaque and easily flakes apart or falls off the bone.

Garnish with fresh cilantro and fresh green chili peppers and serve with plain rice.

═ TIP ═

You could use raw scallops, shrimp, or diced eggplant for this dish; just simmer until cooked through.

CARIBBEAN CHICKEN & MANGO CURRY

SERVES 4
PREP TIME: 25 MINS • COOK TIME: 50 MINS
WF • GF • DF • NF • SoF

2 tablespoons **neutral cooking oil**

1 **onion**, finely diced

1 clove of **garlic**, crushed

a pinch of **salt**

1-inch piece of **ginger**, peeled and finely grated

1 **carrot**, finely diced

1 teaspoon **tomato paste**

2 teaspoons **hot** or **mild Jamaican curry powder** (make mild curry powder hotter by adding ¼ teaspoon **chili powder**)

1¼ pounds skinless, boneless **chicken thighs** or **breasts**, cut into bite-size pieces

¾ cup hot **chicken stock**

1 **Scotch bonnet chili pepper**, left whole, or 2 **red chili peppers**, slit down one side

3 sprigs **thyme**

1 medium **potato**, peeled and cut into ¾-inch cubes

1¾ cups **coconut milk**, from a well-shaken can

½–1 **mango** (depending on size and sweetness), peeled and cut into ¾-inch pieces

Coconut Rice 'n' Peas (see page 178) or **plain rice**, to serve

Make this as hot as you can handle by using a Scotch bonnet chili—the coconut and mango smooth out this curry's fiery edges.

Heat the oil in a large deep saucepan with a lid, set over a medium heat. Add the onion and cook for about 8 minutes, until beginning to soften and brown. Add a generous pinch of salt along with the garlic, ginger, carrot, and tomato paste, and cook for 1 minute, stirring, then add the curry powder. Cook, stirring all the time, for 2 minutes, then add the chicken and sauté for 4 minutes, thoroughly coating it in the spice mixture.

Pour the stock into the pan, add the chili peppers, thyme, and potato and bring to a simmer. Cover and cook until the chicken is cooked through and the potato is tender, about 20–25 minutes. Pour in the coconut milk and add the mango pieces, then stir well and bring back to a simmer.

Taste for salt and spice and remove the chili peppers if it is fiery enough for you, or add a pinch of chili powder if not. Remove the chili peppers and thyme sprigs before serving. Serve with coconut rice and peas, or plain rice.

≡ TIP ≡

This is also good with lamb—add it with the chili peppers and thyme but, since it will take 1½–2 hours to become tender, add a little more liquid, and wait until the last 25 minutes to add the potatoes.

MILD

COLOMBO DE MARTINIQUE

SERVES 4
PREP TIME: 20 MINS • COOK TIME: 53 MINS
WF • GF • DF • NF • SoF (check stock)

2 tablespoons **neutral cooking oil**

1 **onion**, finely diced

1 **red bell pepper**, deseeded and chopped
into ½-inch pieces

2 cloves of **garlic**, crushed

2 teaspoons **hot** or **mild Caribbean/
Jamaican curry powder** + ¼ teaspoon
ground cloves, or 2¼ teaspoons
Colombo curry powder

1¼ pounds boneless, skinless **chicken
thighs** or **breasts**, cut into chunks

1¾ cups hot **chicken** or **vegetable stock**

2 medium **potatoes**, peeled and diced

1 **bay leaf**

3 sprigs **thyme**

2 sprigs **flat-leaf parsley**

1 **Scotch bonnet chili pepper**, left whole,
or 2 **green** or **red chili peppers**, slit
down one side

a generous pinch of **salt**

1 **zucchini**, cut into rough ¾-inch pieces

2 teaspoons **freshly squeezed lime juice**,
to serve

steamed rice, to serve

This recipe comes from the French Caribbean, but is thought to have originated in Sri Lanka. Colombo curry powder is very similar to other more readily available Caribbean curry powders, except it contains cloves, so we mix the two together.

Heat the oil in a large deep saucepan set over a medium heat, add the onion, and cook for about 8 minutes, until beginning to soften and brown. Add the bell pepper and garlic and cook for 1 minute, then add the curry powder and ground cloves, if needed, and cook for 1 minute, stirring. Add the chicken and sauté for 3–4 minutes, thoroughly coating it in the spice mixture.

Add the stock, potatoes, bay leaf, thyme, parsley, and chili pepper, along with a good pinch of salt. Bring to a simmer and cook for 25 minutes (if the pan seems dry, add more water). When the chicken is tender, add the zucchini and cook for 6–8 minutes, until tender but not mushy.

Remove from the heat and taste for salt. Remove and discard the whole chili peppers, parsley and thyme sprigs, and bay leaf. Squeeze over the lime juice and stir through, but be careful, as the lime shouldn't be overwhelming.

Serve with steamed rice.

=== **TIP** ===

Sometimes, Colombo is made with
coconut milk rather than stock, or a
50:50 mix of the two.

CAPE MALAY CURRIED BEEF

SERVES 4
PREP TIME: 20 MINS • COOK TIME: 3½ HOURS
WF • GF • DF • NF • SoF (check rotis) **• SUITABLE FOR FREEZING**

1 tablespoon **neutral cooking oil**

1¾ pounds **chuck steak**, diced and patted dry with paper towel

2 **onions**, finely chopped

5 cloves of **garlic**, crushed

1½-inch piece of **ginger**, peeled and finely grated

3 **red chili peppers** (deseeded or not, to taste), finely chopped

1 **red bell pepper**, deseeded and diced

2 tablespoons **tomato paste**

3 cups **hot water**, or more as needed

1 tablespoon **apple cider vinegar**

2 **bay leaves**

1-inch stick of **cinnamon**

6 **green cardamom pods**

2 sprigs **thyme**

3 ounces **dried apricots**, chopped

salt and **freshly ground black pepper**

fresh cilantro, to garnish (optional)

rotis or **plain rice**, to serve

═ TIP ═

This is often cooked with cubed potatoes added for the last half hour of cooking.

This is a South African curry with a long and sorrowful history. It was created by slave communities, made up of people brought to the Cape from Malaysia and across Asia. Part stew, part curry, the signature feature of a Cape Malay curry is its sweet sharpness, alongside warming spices such as cinnamon.

Heat the oil in a large, deep, heavy saucepan with a tight-fitting lid over a high heat. Add the beef and sear briskly until brown all over, stirring continuously. Remove from the pan with a slotted spoon and set aside.

Add the onions to the pan, reduce the heat to medium, and cook until nicely browned and softened, about 10–15 minutes (test a piece of onion with a spoon—it shouldn't be firm). If the juices seem to be sticking, reduce the heat to low, add 1–2 tablespoons of water, and let it bubble away to deglaze the pan.

Add the garlic, ginger, chili peppers, and bell pepper and cook for 2–3 minutes, stirring. Add the tomato paste and cook, stirring, for a further 2 minutes. Return the meat to the pan and add the water, vinegar, bay leaves, cinnamon stick, green cardamom pods, and thyme. Season, then cover with the lid and cook on the lowest possible heat for 1 hour.

Remove and discard the cinnamon, add the chopped dried apricots, and top up the liquid with more hot water, if needed. Continue to cook, stirring every 30 minutes, for a further 2 hours, or until the meat is melting into the curry sauce.

Remove the bay leaves and thyme sprigs before serving. Taste and add more salt, if needed. Serve garnished with cilantro leaves, with rotis or rice.

FIERY

HEARTBREAK CURRY

SERVES 4

PREP TIME: 20 MINS (PLUS OPTIONAL 2 HOURS MARINATING) • COOK TIME: AT LEAST 1¾ HOURS

WF • GF • DF • NF • SoF (check stock) • SUITABLE FOR FREEZING

1 tablespoon **mild curry powder** (ideally Jamaican)

1½ pounds (2 pounds if bone-in) **goat** or **lamb**, trimmed and cut into chunks

1 large **onion**, finely sliced

1 tablespoon **neutral cooking oil**

2 teaspoons **tomato paste**

2 ounces **tomatoes**, deseeded and finely chopped

4 sprigs **thyme**

1 **Scotch bonnet chili pepper**, whole with a small slit cut into it (handle with care)

4 **allspice berries**

1 **red bell pepper**, deseeded and cut into small chunks

2 cloves of **garlic**, crushed

2 cups hot **chicken** or **vegetable stock**

9 ounces **waxy** or **new potatoes**, cut into small chunks

2 **scallions**, roughly chopped

salt and **freshly ground black pepper**

Coconut Rice 'n' Peas (see page 178), to serve

Rebecca Di Mambro, who works in the marketing team at LEON, reckons this Caribbean curried goat is so hot it counts as a heartbreak curry—that is, the perfect post-breakup curry. "What? I'm not crying. It's just that this curry is terribly spicy."

Goat is a fairly sustainable meat, so it's worth seeking out online or in Caribbean food stores, but you can use lamb or mutton instead. We also created a plantain version of this in our Fast Vegan book—look for fruit with a good covering of brown spots, peel and slice into ½-inch chunks, then simmer in the curry for an hour or until tender.

Combine the curry powder, meat, and onion in a large bowl and use your hands to rub the curry powder in well. It can be marinated for a few hours in the fridge, if you have time, or you can cook right away.

Heat the oil in a large heavy saucepan with a lid over a medium heat. When shimmering hot, add the meat and onions and any leftover curry powder, mix well so that it is well coated in oil, then cover with the lid. Cook for 4–5 minutes, then stir and re-cover. Repeat, stirring every couple of minutes, for a further 10 minutes, until the mixture is slightly browned and the meat is releasing juices into the pan.

Add the tomato paste and cook for 3 minutes, stirring, then add the tomatoes, thyme, Scotch bonnet chili pepper, allspice berries, red bell pepper, and garlic, and cook, gently stirring, for a further 3 minutes. Add the stock and bring to a simmer, then cover with the lid, reduce the heat to low, and cook for 1 hour.

After this time, taste the broth—if the chili pepper has already given it plenty of lip-tingling sour heat, remove and discard it. If not, leave it in (but be warned, it may fall apart and disappear into the curry!). Add a little salt and pepper, if needed (some Jamaican curry powders already contain both). If the meat feels as though it is almost done—and it probably won't just yet, but it's important to check the heat levels at this point—stir in the potatoes and scallions, re-cover, and cook for a final 30 minutes. If the meat still feels very firm, continue to cook the curry, covered, for an hour or even longer, tasting the meat before adding the potatoes and scallions. When the time is up, the potatoes should be tender and the meat falling apart.

Serve with coconut rice 'n' peas.

═ TIP ═

How long the meat will take to cook can vary quite a bit, depending on the cut of meat and the age of the animal, as well as whether you use goat or lamb. Bone-in cuts may take even longer than stated here. This is one for cooking when you have plenty of time, and won't come to harm being left to simmer on low for hours, as long as you keep the liquid levels topped up.

≡ TIP ≡

Pork is commonly served in red curry in Thailand, but you can use vegetables, fish, seafood, or chicken, if you prefer. The crushed red pepper can be substituted with Thai dried mild red spur chili peppers, in which case use double or even triple the amount, to taste.

THAI RED CURRY WITH CRISPY PORK BELLY

SERVES 4
PREP TIME: 25 MINS • COOK TIME: 30 MINS
WF • GF • DF • NF • SoF

1½ pounds **pork belly**, cut into 1-inch chunks

a generous pinch of **fine salt**

vegetable oil, for frying

1¾ cups **coconut milk**

5 ounces **Chinese long beans**, trimmed and sliced into 1-inch pieces

leaves from 2 sprigs **Thai basil**, to garnish

4 **lime wedges**, to serve

sticky rice, to serve

FOR THE CURRY PASTE:

6 **lime leaves**, finely chopped

1 **red chili pepper** (deseeded or not)

1 clove of **garlic**, finely chopped

1 **shallot**, finely chopped

1 teaspoon **galangal paste**

2 teaspoons **fish sauce**

½ teaspoon **ground cumin**

½ teaspoon **ground coriander**

a generous grinding of **black pepper**

1 stick of **lemongrass**, peeled, base trimmed, and finely diced

½ teaspoon **crushed red pepper**

1 tablespoon **very finely chopped cilantro root** or **stalks** (optional)

Often, pork belly is brined, simmered, and then roasted for a crispy result, so this is a total cheat—we just deep-fry it in little nuggets, then plunge it into the red curry at the last minute, for maximum crunch.

Sprinkle the salt over the pork and set aside for 10–15 minutes.

Pour about 1 inch of oil into a deep, high-sided skillet and heat until it reaches 350°F or until a cube of bread browns in 30 seconds .

Pat the pork dry with paper towel. Using tongs, add 3 or 4 chunks of pork at a time to the hot oil (if you have a splatter screen for your pan, use it). Fry for 5–7 minutes, turning once or twice, until golden and crispy. Remove to drain on paper towel and keep warm.

Use a mortar and pestle, blender, or spice grinder to blitz all the paste ingredients until smooth—the best way is in a mortar and pestle but this will take a while.

Heat 1 tablespoon of vegetable oil in a large heavy saucepan over a low heat, add the spice paste, and cook for 3–4 minutes, until fragrant. Add about two-thirds of the coconut milk and slowly increase the heat to bring to a simmer (don't rush or the coconut milk may separate). Add the remaining coconut milk and the beans, and cook until the beans are just tender, about 4–5 minutes.

Taste for salt or chili pepper heat and adjust if needed. Just before serving, add the pork to heat through, but do this as late as you can or it will lose its crunch. Garnish with Thai basil leaves, and serve with lime wedges and sticky rice.

GREEN CURRY AKA GAP YEAR CURRY

SERVES 4

PREP TIME: 20–25 MINS • COOK TIME: UP TO 30 MINS

WF • GF • DF • V • Ve (if using seaweed powder or salt) • NF • SoF (if not using tofu, seitan, mock duck)

2 x 13½-ounce cans **coconut milk**, unshaken

8 **lime leaves**

10½ ounces **mixed vegetables** (choose from **Thai eggplant**, **purple eggplant**, **sweet potato**, **squash** of any kind, sliced **greens**, **baby corn**, **Chinese long beans**, shredded **canned unripe green jackfruit**, thinly sliced **canned bamboo shoots**, **bell peppers**, **snow peas** or **sugar snap peas**), cut into bite-size pieces, as necessary

1½ pounds **protein** (choose from **boneless chicken**, **steak**, **fish**, **seafood**, **browned tofu**, **browned seitan/wheat meat** or **vegan mock duck**), cut into bite-size pieces or strips, as necessary

up to ½ cup **hot water**

leaves from 2–3 sprigs of **Thai basil**

1 **red chili pepper**, thinly sliced on an angle

extra **fish sauce** or **salt**, to taste

Thai jasmine rice, to serve

FOR THE CURRY PASTE (MAKES ABOUT ¼ CUP):

4 medium **green chili peppers**, very finely chopped

The famous Thai green curry gets its color from the green chilies in its freshly made paste—not from herbs, as many people think. You can use 3–4 tablespoons of good-quality ready-made curry paste instead, if you prefer. Add whatever mix of protein and vegetables you fancy.

Green curry and other Thai dishes have made regular appearances on the LEON menu over the years—they are a favorite with John and his family (see page 47). We find the mixture of creamy coconut, salty, hot, sour and almost sweet curry sauce to be irresistible, and this recipe has become a bit of a weeknight regular, especially since you can make it meaty, fishy or plant-based.

Make the paste in either a mortar and pestle or small blender, although the best results do come from pounding it by hand. We often cheat and blitz it first and then finish off with the mortar and pestle to really get the flavors to blossom. Either way, pound the paste ingredients to a smooth paste and look for the oils to be released.

Spoon 1 tablespoon of the thick cream from the top of one of the coconut milk cans into a large deep saucepan, set over a medium heat. Let it melt and begin to sizzle, then add the paste and fry for at least 5 minutes, or until the bright green oil is released and the paste thickens rather than looking wet. Once it smells fragrant, add the remaining coconut milk and the lime leaves and gently bring to a simmer. You will see dots of green oil on the surface—a good thing.

RECIPE CONTINUES ➞

3 **shallots**, very finely chopped

4 cloves of **garlic**, crushed

1½ teaspoons **galangal paste**

1 **lemongrass stalk**, outer layer removed, very finely chopped

½ teaspoon **ground coriander**

½ teaspoon **ground cumin**

2 tablespoons very finely chopped **cilantro root** or **stalks**

1 teaspoon **fish sauce** or ½ teaspoon **Thai shrimp paste** (or **seaweed powder**)

freshly ground black pepper, to taste

If adding vegetables that need more cooking than your chosen protein (such as butternut squash), add them now and cook until just tender, before adding the protein. Chicken pieces will need about 20 minutes, but salmon, tofu, and crisp vegetables like green beans will only need a few minutes in the broth. If you find there isn't enough liquid to cover everything in the pan, add the water and bring back to a simmer.

Once everything is cooked to your liking, remove from the heat and add the Thai basil leaves and chili pepper. Taste the broth and add more fish sauce or salt, as needed (depending on how salty your fish sauce is, if using, you might need up to 2 more teaspoons).

Serve with Thai jasmine rice.

=== TIP ===

You can cook bone-in chicken in this (or even a whole chicken, chopped into small pieces), but poach in boiling water for about 20 minutes before placing it in the curry, and use its cooking liquid instead of the hot water.

JOHN'S THAI FOOD DISCOVERY

"The first Thai food I ever ate was at university. A basement café opened up opposite my halls of residence, and it was probably the only Thai restaurant in town, way back in 1993. I don't think younger people necessarily realize how scarce Asian food was then—it wasn't at all common to be able to get a really good curry. This place did all the classic stuff, like green curry, and I ate there as much as I could, all the way through university.

Later, I started cooking a lot of Thai food myself, after Katie and I went backpacking to Bangkok and Chiang Mai, and then on to Koh Samui and Koh Tao. Eating Thai food on the beach in Thailand was just one of the most amazing things. That's why I now insist on putting Thai curries on the LEON menu—they are a very powerful food memory for me."

≡ TIP ≡

Chicken thighs have
more flavor, but use
chicken breast if you want a
neater-looking curry.

JUNGLE CURRY

SERVES 4

PREP TIME: 30 MINS • COOK TIME: 25 MINS

WF • GF • DF • NF • SoF

2–3 tablespoons **neutral cooking oil**

1 pound **eggplant**, cut into ¾-inch cubes

2½ cups hot **chicken stock**

8–10 **lime leaves**

1¾ pounds skinless, boneless **chicken thighs**, cut into bite-size pieces

5 ounces **Chinese long beans**

5 ounces **baby corn**

leaves from 4 sprigs **Thai basil**

freshly squeezed lime juice, to taste

salt, to taste

Thai jasmine or **sticky rice**, to serve

FOR THE CURRY PASTE:

2 medium **shallots**, finely chopped

1–2 **red chili peppers** (deseeded or not, to taste)

1 **lemongrass stalk**, outer layer removed, finely chopped

1-inch piece of **ginger**, peeled and finely grated

3 cloves of **garlic**, crushed

½ teaspoon **crushed red pepper**

2 teaspoons **fish sauce**

½ teaspoon **galangal paste**

1 tablespoon **very finely chopped cilantro root** or **stalks** (optional)

½ teaspoon **ground coriander**

This Northern Thai curry is made without coconut (in the past, very few coconut palms grew in Northern Thailand). You can now buy jungle curry paste, if you don't have time to make it fresh.

Grind all the curry paste ingredients together until fairly smooth, using a mortar and pestle, spice grinder, or small blender (or use about 3 tablespoons of a good-quality, ready-made jungle curry paste).

Heat 2 tablespoons of the oil in a large saucepan with a lid, set over a medium heat, add the spice paste, and fry for 2–3 minutes, until really fragrant. Add the eggplant, plus the remaining oil if needed, and sauté for 4–5 minutes, stirring frequently so the paste doesn't stick and burn. Stir in the hot stock and lime leaves, scraping up any paste stuck to the bottom and sides of the pan, and bring to a simmer. Add the chicken, partly cover with a lid, and cook for 8 minutes, stirring once or twice.

Add the beans and baby corn, pushing them into the curry until submerged, then cover completely with the lid and simmer for 3 minutes. If the curry looks very thin (it should be soupy), remove the lid and increase the heat for a final 3–4 minutes. Remove from the heat and stir in most of the Thai basil, plus a good squeeze or two of lime juice. Taste for salt (or fish sauce or chili pepper), adding more as needed.

Divide the curry among 4 bowls. Garnish with the remaining Thai basil leaves and serve with rice on the side.

PORK VINDALOO ·

SERVES 4
PREP TIME: 20 MINS, PLUS 2–12 HOURS MARINATING • COOK TIME: 1 HOUR 10 MINS
WF • GF • DF • NF • SoF • SUITABLE FOR FREEZING

2 pounds **pork shoulder**, fat trimmed, cut into large chunks

2 tablespoons **neutral cooking oil** or **ghee**

3 **onions**, finely sliced

1 teaspoon **mustard seeds**

1 teaspoon **tamarind paste** or **concentrate** (optional)

steamed rice, to serve

FOR THE MARINADE:
5 **cloves**

seeds from 6 **cardamom pods**

1 teaspoon **coriander seeds**

½ teaspoon **cumin seeds**

½ teaspoon **ground turmeric**

2 teaspoons **sweet paprika** (the reddest you can find)

¼ teaspoon **ground cinnamon**

¼ teaspoon **freshly ground black pepper**

½ teaspoon **chili powder**

2 teaspoons **crushed red pepper** (or more for a really fiery vindaloo)

5 cloves of **garlic**, crushed

1-inch piece of **ginger**, peeled and finely grated

3 tablespoons **red wine vinegar**

a generous pinch of **salt**

One of Rebecca's happiest holidays was traveling around south India with her now-husband Steve. They had no money and slept in beach huts, and it was wonderful. This hot-and-sour Goan-style vindaloo was created by Goan cooks and Portuguese colonialists centuries ago, when Goa was part of Portugal's vast empire. It comes from vinha d'alhos, a Portuguese meat stew made with vinegar.

To make the marinade, grind the whole spices to a powder in a mortar and pestle or spice grinder. Mix in the ground spices, chili powder, and crushed red pepper, then mix in the garlic, ginger, vinegar, and salt until well combined.

Use your hands to work the marinade into the pork, then cover and chill in the fridge for at least 2 hours or overnight.

When ready to cook, heat the oil in a large heavy saucepan over a medium-high heat. Add the onions and cook for 10–12 minutes, stirring often, until the onions are golden. Add the mustard seeds and cook until they begin to crackle, 1–2 minutes. Add the marinated pork along with the marinade and cook for 5 minutes, stirring. Add ¾ cup hot water and stir well, scraping up anything that has stuck to the pan, and bring to a boil. Reduce the heat and gently simmer, uncovered, for 45 minutes, stirring every 10 minutes or so.

About 10 minutes before the end of cooking, stir through the tamarind concentrate, if using.

Taste for salt and chili pepper heat levels and adjust if necessary. If the sauce is still quite loose, increase the heat and allow it to reduce—a vindaloo should have a thick, rich gravy. Serve with steamed rice.

≡ TIP ≡

Don't worry about
the amount of vinegar
used here—although this is a
piquant curry, it doesn't taste
of vinegar.

BEEF MADRAS

SERVES 4

PREP TIME: 15 MINS • COOK TIME: 3½ HOURS

WF • GF • DF (if using oil) • NF • SoF • SUITABLE FOR FREEZING

2 tablespoons **neutral cooking oil** or **ghee**

2 **onions**, finely diced

1 medium **carrot**, very finely diced

3 cloves of **garlic**, crushed

1½-inch piece of **ginger**, peeled and grated

½–1 medium **green chili pepper**
    (deseeded or not, to taste)

1½ teaspoons **chili powder**

1 heaped teaspoon **Madras curry powder**

1 teaspoon **paprika**

1½ teaspoons **ground cumin**

1 teaspoon **ground coriander**

1 teaspoon **ground turmeric**

2¼ cups **hot water**, plus extra as needed

7 ounces **tomato purée**

1¾ pounds **chuck steak**, cut into bite-size
    pieces

2 teaspoons good-quality **apple cider
    vinegar**

salt and **freshly ground black pepper**

plain or **pilau rice**, to serve

Raita (see page 164), to serve

The Madras curry is a British curry house invention (not a bad thing) and has come to mean a very hot curry in a slow-cooked tomato-based sauce. Here is our favorite version.

Heat the oil or ghee in a large heavy saucepan with a lid, set over a medium-high heat. Add the onions and carrot and sauté until the onions are translucent and beginning to brown, 8–10 minutes. Add the garlic, ginger, and chili pepper and cook for 2–3 minutes, until fragrant, but don't allow the mixture to stick and burn. Add the ground spices and cook, stirring, for 1 minute, then add ½ cup of the water and mix to form a paste. Cook for about 5 minutes, until the water has evaporated, then add the tomato purée and cook for 3–4 minutes, stirring.

Stir in the beef, remaining hot water, and vinegar, and season well with salt and black pepper, then cover with the lid and bring to a gentle simmer. Reduce the heat to low and cook, covered, for 2–3 hours. Stir the curry occasionally so that nothing sticks to the bottom of the pan, and top up with water if necessary.

When the meat is meltingly tender and beginning to fall apart, remove the lid, turn the heat to medium, and let the sauce reduce until it is very thick and coats each piece of meat. If you want a smooth sauce, use tongs to remove the meat and process the sauce to a purée with an immersion blender, then return the meat to the pan.

Serve with plain or pilau rice and raita, or as part of a spread of curries with dhal and flatbreads.

═ TIP ═

For that true curry house flavor, add a dollop of ghee to the finished curry and stir through, just before serving.

CHIARA'S GRANDMOTHER'S GOAN-STYLE CHICKEN CAFREAL

SERVES 4

PREP TIME: 20 MINS, PLUS 12 HOURS MARINATING • COOK TIME: 45–55 MINS

WF • GF • DF • NF • SoF

4–8 (depending on size and hunger) skinless, bone-in **chicken thighs**

2 tablespoons **neutral cooking oil**

2-inch stick of **cinnamon**

4 **green cardamom pods**

5 **black peppercorns**

2 **onions**, diced

½ teaspoon each **ground cumin**, **ground coriander**, and **cumin seeds**

¼ teaspoon **ground turmeric**

1 tablespoon **desiccated coconut**

salt and **freshly ground black pepper**

cilantro leaves and **rice** or **Indian flatbreads** (see pages 198–201), to serve

FOR THE MARINADE:

½ **onion**, diced

a handful of **fresh cilantro**, finely chopped

1-inch piece of **ginger**, peeled and grated

6 cloves of **garlic**, finely chopped

4 **green chili peppers** (deseeded or not, to taste), finely chopped

1 heaped teaspoon **coriander seeds**

1 tablespoon **apple cider vinegar**

LEON regular Chiara Pinto sent us this favorite family recipe. "This has a green masala that coats the meat as a thick sauce—if you want more sauce you can add more water or even coconut milk. It was my grandmother's recipe and she added roasted coconut to thicken the sauce. We serve it with a soft bread called pao, but rice is good too."

To make the marinade, grind the ingredients to a paste in a mortar and pestle or spice grinder. Make a couple of slashes in the thicker parts of the chicken thighs, then massage the paste into the meat. Cover and marinate in the fridge overnight.

When ready to cook, heat the oil in a large saucepan with a lid, over a medium heat. Add the cinnamon, cardamom pods, and peppercorns, and fry for 3 minutes, to flavor the oil. Remove from the pan, leaving the oil behind. Add the onions and cook for 6–8 minutes, stirring, until translucent. Add the ground spices and cumin seeds and fry for 1 minute. Stir in the chicken, its marinade, and a splash of water, then cover with the lid and cook for 20 minutes, stirring regularly and adding 3–4 tablespoons of water every now and then, to stop it sticking. Meanwhile, in a small dry skillet over a medium heat, toast the coconut until golden. Tip out of the pan immediately and grind to a fine powder in a mortar and pestle.

Add the coconut and some salt and pepper to the pan, re-cover, and cook for a further 10–25 minutes, depending on the size of the chicken thighs, until done (pierce the meat to the bone—the juices should run clear).

To serve, sprinkle with a little fresh cilantro, and eat with rice or flatbreads.

CARIBBEAN-STYLE BLACK BEAN CURRY

SERVES 2 AS A MAIN OR 4 AS A SIDE
PREP TIME: 20 MINS • COOK TIME: 25 MINS
WF • GF • DF • V • Ve • NF • SoF (check rotis) • **SUITABLE FOR FREEZING**

1 tablespoon **neutral cooking oil**

1 **onion**, finely chopped

½ **red** or **orange bell pepper**, deseeded and diced

2 cloves of **garlic**, crushed

¾-inch piece of **ginger**, peeled and finely grated

10 sprigs of **fresh cilantro**, stalks finely chopped, leaves reserved to garnish

1 teaspoon **mild** or **medium curry powder** (ideally Jamaican but Madras or similar will work)

¼ teaspoon **chili powder** (optional)

15-ounce can **black beans in water**, undrained

1 sprig of **thyme**

1 **bay leaf**

2 tablespoons **coconut milk** or **coconut cream**

½ teaspoon **apple cider vinegar**

salt and **freshly ground black pepper**

1 **shallot**, finely sliced, to garnish

freshly squeezed lime juice, to serve

rice or **Rotis** (see page 200), to serve

Don't skip the toppings—the shallot and lime really make this curry sing.

Heat the oil in a saucepan set over a medium heat, add the onion and pepper, and sauté for about 8 minutes, until softened and the onion is just beginning to brown. Add the garlic, ginger, cilantro stalks, curry powder, and chili powder, if using. Cook, stirring, for 2–3 minutes, until fragrant. Add the beans along with the water from the can, the thyme, and bay leaf and bring to a simmer, then reduce the heat to low and gently simmer for 10 minutes, stirring every now and then (add a splash of water if the pan gets too dry).

Remove from the heat and add the coconut milk or coconut cream and the vinegar. Stir well, then taste for salt and pepper—add a touch more vinegar if you'd like more tang.

To serve, divide among bowls, then top each one with the reserved cilantro leaves, sliced shallot, and a little squeeze of lime juice. Eat with rice or roti, as a main, or alongside jerk chicken or tofu.

═ TIP ═

If you really like to make your tongue tingle, swap the green chili pepper for ¼ of a super-hot Scotch bonnet pepper, deseeded and finely diced (be sure to wash your hands or wear gloves).

CREAMY

SAG PANEER

SERVES 2 AS A MAIN OR 4 AS A SIDE
PREP TIME: 15 MINS • COOK TIME: 35 MINS
WF • GF • V • Ve (with substitutions, see tip) • NF • SoF

1 pound **spinach leaves**, large stems removed, leaves roughly chopped

2 ounces **frozen fenugreek leaves**, defrosted (optional)

2 tablespoons **ghee** or **vegetable oil**

9 ounces **paneer** (a firm Indian curd cheese), cut into rough ¾-inch cubes, patted dry with paper towel

1 **onion**, finely sliced

a pinch of **salt**

3 cloves of **garlic**, crushed

¾-inch piece of **ginger**, peeled and finely grated

1 teaspoon **garam masala**

½ teaspoon **turmeric**

a pinch of **cumin seeds**

a pinch of **freshly grated nutmeg**

a pinch of **crushed red pepper** (optional)

3–4 tablespoons **heavy cream**

a handful of **fresh cilantro**, roughly chopped (optional)

freshly squeezed lemon juice, to taste

Once upon a time, Rebecca was a vegetarian. Her student house had a Wednesday ritual of watching Sex and the City *(the first series!) and getting a takeaway. This gloriously rich and creamy curry house favorite was always her order. In India, you might find it made without the cream, in which case a dollop of ghee, melted in at the end, is a good idea.*

Wash the spinach, then tip the wet leaves into a large saucepan with a lid, set over a medium heat. Steam along with the fenugreek leaves, if using, for 4–5 minutes, until the spinach has just wilted (work in batches if necessary). Drain and cool in a colander set over the sink.

Heat the ghee or oil in a large wide skillet with a lid over a medium heat. When the ghee has melted, carefully add the paneer (it may splatter). Cook for just 1 minute or so on each side, then turn—you want it to be golden, but not dry. Use tongs to remove from the pan and set aside. Reduce the heat to low and add the onions to the pan, along with a pinch of salt. Cook for about 10 minutes, stirring, until soft and barely browned. Add the garlic, ginger, garam masala, turmeric, and cumin seeds and cook for 3–4 minutes, stirring often.

Gently squeeze the excess water out of the cooled spinach (not too thoroughly, but it mustn't be soggy) and add it, along with the cooked paneer, to the pan. Add the nutmeg, crushed red pepper, if using, and 3 tablespoons of the cream, and cook briefly, stirring until well combined.

Remove from the heat and stir in the cilantro leaves, if using, and squeeze over a little lemon juice. Taste and decide if you want to add more crushed red pepper, cream, lemon, or salt. Serve immediately.

= TIP =

Vegans can use
vegetable oil or vegan
ghee, leave out the cream,
and substitute the paneer
for tofu, cooked in the
same way.

━ TIP ━

To make this more filling, add cooked chickpeas or cooked lentils when adding the beets. If you have any Sri Lankan roasted curry powder (see page 106), a pinch on top of the finished curry works wonders.

BEET & COCONUT CURRY

1 tablespoon **neutral cooking oil**

½ teaspoon **mustards seeds**

1 teaspoon **cumin seeds**

a pinch of **fenugreek seeds**

½ **onion**, finely sliced

¾-inch piece of **ginger**, peeled and finely grated

2 cloves of **garlic**, crushed

1 medium **green chili pepper**, finely chopped

½ teaspoon **ground coriander**

14 ounces **beets**, peeled, quartered, and sliced into ¼-inch pieces

½ cup **water**

1 cup **coconut milk**

1 tablespoon **desiccated coconut**

1 teaspoon finely chopped **red chili pepper**

1 tablespoon **finely chopped fresh cilantro**

zest of ½ a **lime**

2 teaspoons **freshly squeezed lime juice**, or more to taste

salt and **freshly ground black pepper**

Earthy beetroot makes this curry almost sweet, but it is bolstered by chili heat, sour lime and the coconut crunch of the topping.

Heat the oil in a large saucepan with a lid, set over a medium heat. Add the mustard seeds and, when they start to pop, add the cumin and fenugreek seeds and cook for 1 minute. Add the onion and cook for 5 minutes, then add the ginger, garlic, and green chili pepper and cook, stirring, for 3–4 minutes. Add the ground coriander and cook for a further 1 minute.

Add the beets, water, and ¾ cup of the coconut milk and bring to a simmer. Partially cover with the lid, and simmer for about 20 minutes, or until the beets are just tender.

Meanwhile, make the topping. Set a small dry saucepan over a medium heat and add the desiccated coconut. Cook for 1–2 minutes, moving it around the pan just until it begins to brown, then immediately transfer it to a small bowl. Add the chopped red chili pepper, cilantro, and lime zest, along with a pinch of salt, and mix well.

When the beets are tender, add the remaining ¼ cup of coconut milk to the curry and just warm through a little. Remove from the heat and season to taste with lime juice and plenty of salt and freshly ground black pepper.

Serve each bowlful topped with a sprinkling of the toasted coconut mixture.

SHUMAIYA'S FAMILY CHICKEN KORMA

SERVES 8–10

PREP TIME: 20 MINS • COOK TIME: 1 HOUR

WF • GF • NF • SoF (check pilau/paratha)

4 tablespoons **ghee**

3 **onions**, finely sliced

1 teaspoon **pink Himalayan salt**, or
  ¾ teaspoon ordinary **salt**

2-inch stick of **cinnamon**, roughly broken

½ teaspoon **cumin seeds**

3–5 **cloves**

3 **bay leaves**

4 **green cardamom pods**

½ teaspoon **black peppercorns**

1 teaspoon **ground white pepper**

3 cloves of **garlic**, minced

1½-inch piece of **ginger**, peeled and finely
  grated

3–5 **green chili peppers**, split lengthways,
  to taste

3-pound **whole chicken**, cut into jointed
  portions on the bone, skin removed
  (or use the same weight of **thighs** and
  drumsticks)

10 **eggs**, at room temperature

a handful of **fresh cilantro**, to garnish
  (optional)

Pilau (made without meat, see page 177)
  or **Paratha** (see page 205), to serve

When John gets takeaway, he orders curry from Nizam in Haywards Heath, and he doesn't even need to ask what his kids want: korma.

Our friend Shumi (or Shumaiya)'s family is from Bangladesh. "A Bengali kulma (aka korma) is buttery and rich, and quite unlike what most of Britain knows as a korma. Its natural sweetness comes from slow-cooked onions and whole spices. Made for special occasions, this recipe has been passed down from generation to generation."

Heat the ghee in a very large heavy saucepan with a lid, set over a medium-low heat. Add the onions, salt, spices, bay leaves, cardamom pods, and black and white pepper. Cook until softened and slightly translucent, 10–15 minutes.

Add the garlic, ginger, and chili peppers, and cook until the onions are on the verge of becoming jam-like and the oil separates from the mixture, about 10 minutes.

Increase the heat to medium and add the chicken, including the carcass. Stir, then cover with the lid and reduce the heat to low. Cook for 30 minutes, stirring occasionally, until the chicken is thoroughly cooked and the juices have emulsified to a gravy. Don't let the juices dry up and, if needed, add around ½ cup of water.

After 20 minutes cooking, bring a saucepan of water to the boil, add the eggs, and cook for 7 minutes (don't hard-boil them). Drain and cool under running water, then peel and add to the chicken korma for the final 2 minutes of cooking to warm through.

Check seasoning, adding more as needed. If you used the chicken carcass, remove it now. Garnish with fresh cilantro and serve with a plain (meatless) pilau or freshly cooked, crispy parathas.

TIP

Adding salt to the onions stops them from browning too quickly—a neat trick if you want soft, translucent onions in a dish.

NILGIRI CURRY

SERVES 4

PREP TIME: 25 MINS, PLUS 30 MINS–8 HOURS MARINATING • COOK TIME: 1 HOUR

Can be **WF • GF • DF • NF • SoF**

1¾ pounds skinless, boneless **chicken thighs** or **breasts**, cut into bite-size pieces

6 tablespoons **whole-milk plain yogurt** (or a rich **coconut** or **almond yogurt**)

1 teaspoon **ground turmeric**

1 tablespoon **neutral cooking oil**

2 **onions**, finely chopped

seeds from 7 **green cardamom pods**

4 **cloves**

a large handful of **fresh cilantro**, finely chopped, plus a little to garnish

6 sprigs of **mint**, finely chopped

2 medium **green chili peppers** (deseeded or not), finely chopped

about 1 cup **cold water**, plus extra as needed

1½-inch piece of **ginger**, peeled and finely grated

3 cloves of **garlic**, crushed

a pinch of **fennel seeds**

½ teaspoon **ground cinnamon**

8 **curry leaves**

1 **bay leaf**

1 ounce **unroasted cashew nuts**, chopped

4 tablespoons **coconut milk**

salt

rice or **Chapati** (see page 200), to serve

The Nilgiri mountains are in Southern India. This fragrant green curry, made with heaps of cilantro and mint, is originally from the local hill-station towns. At LEON, we believe in the power of fresh herbs, so this one is right up our street.

Combine the chicken in a bowl with the yogurt, turmeric, and ½ teaspoon of salt. Cover and marinate in the fridge for 30 minutes–8 hours.

Heat the oil in a large wide heavy saucepan over a medium heat. Add the onions and a pinch of salt, and cook for about 8 minutes, stirring, until soft and translucent. Meanwhile, grind the cardamom seeds and cloves to a powder in a mortar and pestle.

Blitz the cilantro, mint, chili peppers, and cold water in a blender to a pesto texture.

Add the ginger, garlic, freshly ground spices, fennel seeds, and ground cinnamon to the pan and cook for 3–4 minutes, stirring, until fragrant. Then, add the herb mixture to the pan, along with the curry leaves, bay leaf, the chicken and all of its marinade, and bring to a simmer.

Grind the cashew nuts in the mortar and pestle, as finely as you can, then add them to the pan, cover, and simmer for 30 minutes. Stir halfway through and add a little water if it is drying out.

At the end of cooking, uncover the pan. If there is a lot of liquid (the herbs will release a little during cooking), increase the heat and let it reduce for 3–5 minutes. Add the coconut milk, then taste and add salt, if needed.

Serve sprinkled with the extra cilantro, with rice or chapati alongside.

LAMB PASANDA

1½ pounds **lamb leg** (steaks or large pieces), cut into thin slices

7 tablespoons **whole-milk plain yogurt**

6 tablespoons **light cream**

5 tablespoons **ground almonds**

1½-inch piece of **ginger**, peeled and finely grated

3 cloves of **garlic**, crushed

1 teaspoon **ground coriander**

1 teaspoon **ground turmeric**

1 teaspoon **paprika**

¼–½ teaspoon **chili powder**, to taste

1 teaspoon **ground cumin**

1 tablespoon **neutral cooking oil**

1 large **onion**, finely sliced

½–1 **green chili pepper** (deseeded or not, to taste), finely chopped

½ teaspoon **cumin seeds**

a pinch of **fenugreek seeds** (optional)

6 **green cardamom pods**

¼ teaspoon **ground cinnamon**

a pinch of **freshly ground nutmeg**

4 **cloves**

salt

2 cups **hot water**

basmati rice, to serve

A creamy and mild curry that you will always, **always,** *find on the menu in British curry houses.*

Arrange the lamb slices in a single layer on a cutting board, cover with plastic wrap, and bash with a rolling pin (or meat mallet) until thin. In a large bowl, mix together 6 tablespoons of the yogurt with the cream, ground almonds, ginger, garlic, and ground spices. Cover and marinate in the fridge for 30 minutes, or overnight.

When ready to cook, heat the oil in a large deep saucepan with a lid over a medium-low heat. Add the onion and gently cook for 10–12 minutes, until browned. Add the chili pepper, cumin seeds, fenugreek seeds, if using, cardamom pods, cinnamon, nutmeg, and cloves, along with a pinch of salt. Cook for about 2 minutes, stirring, until the spices are fragrant.

Add the lamb and all the marinade and cook for 1–2 minutes, stirring, then reduce the heat and add the hot water. Cover and bring to a gentle simmer and cook for 45 minutes, stirring now and then. Remove the lid about halfway through, so that the liquid can reduce.

When the oil rises to the top of the curry, it is ready. Taste a piece of the lamb—it should be very tender. If necessary, increase the heat to reduce the liquid; the curry should be saucy, but not wet. Remove from the heat and stir through the remaining yogurt.

Serve immediately, with rice.

=== TIP ===

Save time by batch-cooking double the quantity of meatballs and then freezing them. If you have any Thai basil (not always easy to find), add a handful of leaves before serving.

CHICKEN MEATBALL COCONUT CURRY

SERVES 4
PREP TIME: 20 MINS • COOK TIME: 33 MINS
WF • GF • DF • NF • SoF

1 tablespoon **neutral cooking oil**

1½ pounds skinless, boneless **chicken thighs** (or **ground chicken** or **turkey**)

2 tablespoons good-quality **Thai red curry paste** (or use the recipe on page 43)

4 **scallions**, finely chopped

2½ cups **coconut milk**

1 clove of **garlic**, crushed

2 teaspoons **fish sauce** (or a good pinch of **salt**)

6 **lime leaves**, torn

1 stick of **lemongrass**, whole, bruised with a rolling pin

½–1 teaspoon **crushed red pepper**, to taste

½ teaspoon **ground coriander**

½ teaspoon **ground cumin**

½ teaspoon **ground turmeric**

4 ounces **Chinese long beans**, trimmed

5 ounces **asparagus**, trimmed and split lengthways

4 ounces **baby corn**, split lengthways

1 head **bok choy**, leaves split lengthways, cut into bite-size pieces

steamed rice or **Thai noodles**, to serve

This is incredibly quick and easy to prepare, but looks and tastes amazing. We were inspired to create this recipe because LEON's Sicilian Meatballs are so popular.

Heat the oven to 400°F and grease a large roasting pan with the oil.

Place the chicken, red curry paste, three-quarters of the scallions, and a pinch of salt in a food processor and blitz to mince the chicken (if using ground chicken or turkey, just mix everything together). Shape the mixture into 20 meatballs, about the size of ping-pong balls. Place in the roasting pan and bake for 10 minutes. Remove from the oven and use tongs to turn each one, then bake for a further 10 minutes.

Meanwhile, in a large bowl, combine the coconut milk, garlic, fish sauce or salt, remaining scallions, lime leaves, lemongrass, crushed red pepper, and ground spices.

Remove the roasting pan from the oven and add the vegetables. Pour over the coconut mixture, then toss everything together. Arrange the meatballs and vegetables roughly in a single layer in the dish, making sure the lime leaves and bok choy leaves are submerged.

Bake for 5 minutes, then remove to shake everything around and turn the meatballs one last time. Return to the oven for a final 8 minutes.

Taste the broth for seasoning. Serve with steamed rice or Thai noodles.

ERICA'S LENTIL MASALA

SERVES 4

PREP TIME: 20 MINS • COOK TIME: 50 MINS

WF • GF • DF • V • Ve • NF • SoF (check stock)

5 ounces **uncooked lentils**

1 tablespoon **neutral cooking oil**

½ teaspoon each **cumin** and **mustard seeds**

1 small **onion**, half finely sliced, half grated

2 cloves of **garlic**, crushed

1 teaspoon **peeled and finely grated ginger**

½ **green chili pepper**, deseeded and finely diced

1 small **carrot**, very finely diced

½ **celery stick**, finely diced

1 teaspoon **ground cumin**

1 teaspoon **ground coriander**

1½ teaspoons **sweet smoked paprika**

2 heaped teaspoons **curry powder**

1 tablespoon **apple cider vinegar**

2 teaspoons **tomato paste**

½ cup **tomato puree** or **tomato sauce**

¾ cup **coconut milk**

¾ cup good-quality **vegetable** or **vegan stock**

½ **butternut squash**, peeled, cut into ½-inch pieces

3 ounces **kale** or **spring greens**, stems and ribs removed, finely shredded

salt and **freshly ground black pepper**

freshly squeezed lemon juice, to serve

brown or **white rice**, to serve

Erica Molyneaux is LEON's head of food (best job title ever?) and created this autumnal vegan recipe for the LEON menu last year. You can use any kind of lentils, but we love chana dal/split yellow gram, as they hold their shape.

Place the uncooked lentils in a saucepan and cover with 2-inch depth of cold water. Bring to a boil, then reduce the heat and simmer until tender but not turning to mush (how long depends on which lentil you choose—red lentils take around 20 minutes; chana dal can take as long as 50 minutes).

Meanwhile, heat the oil in a large deep saucepan with a lid over a medium heat. When hot, add the cumin and mustard seeds. As soon as the mustard seeds start to pop, add the sliced and grated onion, garlic, ginger, chili pepper, carrot, and celery. Cook for 6 minutes, stirring often, until the sliced onion is translucent. Add all the spices and cook for 1 minute, stirring, until fragrant. Mix in ½ cup water, then gently simmer for about 5 minutes, stirring now and then. When the water has evaporated, the mixture seems thick and glossy, and oil is rising to the top, add the vinegar and tomato paste. Cook for 3–4 minutes, then add the tomato puree or sauce, coconut milk, stock, and butternut squash. Bring to a simmer, cover, and cook for 25 minutes, until the squash is done—it should hold its shape, so don't let it overcook.

Taste the curry and add salt and pepper, as needed. For the last 3–4 minutes of cooking, stir through the kale and the cooked lentils.

Serve over rice, with a squeeze of lemon to finish.

≡ TIP ≡

Using bone-in chicken gives
more flavor, but for speed you
can use boneless (use 1¼ pounds and
halve the cooking time). In Thailand,
this is served topped with crunchy
deep-fried noodles. To make your own:
blanch and pat dry an extra 4 ounces
egg noodles, then briefly fry in ¾
inch hot oil, until crisp.

KHAO SOI GAI

SERVES 4

PREP TIME: 20 MINS • COOK TIME: 50 MINS

DF • NF • SoF (check stock)

2 teaspoons **coriander seeds**

seeds from 4 **green cardamom pods**

2 tablespoons **finely grated turmeric root** (optional)

1½-inch piece of **ginger**, peeled and grated

1 tablespoon **very finely chopped cilantro stalks**

4 tablespoons **Thai red curry paste**

1 tablespoon **neutral cooking oil**

2½ cups **coconut milk**

1¾ cup hot **chicken stock**

8 **lime leaves**, roughly torn

1 teaspoon **fish sauce**, or more to taste

2 pounds bone-in **chicken thighs** and **drumsticks** (ideally 8 small pieces), skin on or off

7 ounces **Asian leafy greens**, sliced into 1-inch pieces (we use choy sum)

2½ ounces **dried medium egg noodles**

salt

TO SERVE:

a handful of **fresh cilantro**

crispy onions (bought or homemade, see page 179)

a drizzle of **spicy chili oil** (optional)

lime wedges

This curried noodle soup is from Chiang Mai in Northern Thailand, but is related to dishes found in neighboring Burma. Find turmeric root next to the fresh ginger in large supermarkets.

Grind the dry spices to a powder in a mortar and pestle. Add the turmeric, ginger, and cilantro stalks and pound to a paste. Add the red curry paste and mix well.

Heat the oil in a very large deep heavy saucepan, over a medium heat. When hot, add the spice paste and cook, stirring, for 4–5 minutes, until really fragrant. Reduce the heat to low, add half the coconut milk, and bring to a simmer, then add the rest along with the stock, lime leaves, and fish sauce. Bring to a simmer again. Make a few deep slashes down to the bone in the chicken, then submerge in the broth and cook, covered, for 30 minutes. Halfway through, turn each piece of chicken over to ensure they cook all the way through.

Meanwhile, bring a large saucepan of salted water to a boil.

Check the chicken is done by piercing a thick piece; if the juices run clear, it is cooked (if not, cook for a further 5–10 minutes). Stir the greens into the pan, cover, and cook for 3 minutes.

Blanch the noodles in the boiling water for 2–3 minutes, until al dente. Drain and refresh under a little running cold water so they don't become soggy, and divide among 4 wide shallow bowls.

Taste the curry and add a little more fish sauce if needed. Place 1 or 2 pieces of chicken into each bowl on top of the noodles, then ladle the curry and greens over. Finish with cilantro, some crispy onions, a drizzle of chili oil, and lime wedges.

CHICKEN CHETTINAD

SERVES 4

PREP TIME: 10 MINS, PLUS 1 HOUR MARINATING • COOK TIME: 1 HOUR

WF • GF • SoF (check flatbreads) **• SUITABLE FOR FREEZING**

2½ pounds skinless, boneless **chicken thighs** or **breasts**, cut into large chunks

5 tablespoons **whole-milk plain yogurt**

1½ teaspoons **chili powder** (to taste)

1 teaspoon **sweet paprika**

½ teaspoon **ground turmeric**

1 tablespoon **neutral cooking oil**

2 **onions**, finely sliced

10 **curry leaves**

1-inch piece of **ginger**, peeled and finely grated

3 cloves of **garlic**, crushed

7 ounces **diced tomatoes** (fresh or canned)

salt and **freshly ground black pepper**

a handful of **fresh cilantro**, to garnish

rice or **Indian flatbreads** (see pages 198–201 and 205–206), to serve

FOR THE SPICE BLEND:

1 teaspoon each **cumin** and **coriander seeds**

½ teaspoon **fennel seeds**

4 **cloves**

a pinch of **ground cinnamon**

2 tablespoons **chopped cashew nuts**

seeds from 3 **green cardamom pods**

4 tablespoons **desiccated coconut**

This nifty recipe is from Tamil Nadu in India. Using cashew nuts and desiccated coconut in the sauce makes it rich and thick, without needing buckets of cream.

Place the chicken in a bowl with the yogurt, chili powder, paprika, and turmeric. Mix well, then cover and place in the fridge for at least 1 hour, or as long as overnight.

When ready to cook, set a large skillet over a medium heat. Add all the spice blend ingredients and toast, stirring frequently, for 3–4 minutes, until the spices smell wonderful and the coconut is golden. Tip everything into a spice grinder or mortar and pestle and grind to a fine powder. Add 2 tablespoons water and mix to form a paste.

Heat the oil in a large deep saucepan with a lid over a medium heat. When hot, add the onions and cook, stirring often, until they are beginning to turn golden brown. Add the curry leaves, ginger, and garlic, and sizzle for about 5 minutes, stirring now and then and taking care not to let it burn, then add the tomatoes, and cook, stirring again, for 3–4 minutes. Scrape the chicken and all of its marinade into the pan, then tip in the spice paste and mix. Cook for 2 minutes, then add just enough water to make everything saucy, about ½–¾ cup. Add a good pinch of salt and a generous dusting of black pepper, stir, then cover and cook for about 25 minutes, until the chicken is cooked through and tender. If it seems at all wet, uncover the pan for the last 5 minutes or so of the cooking time.

Garnish with a little fresh cilantro and serve with rice or Indian flatbreads.

≡ TIP ≡

Vegetarians and vegans
can swap the meat for potatoes,
cauliflower, and beans, or any root
vegetables, and the yogurt for coconut
or almond yogurt. The sauce is robust,
so if you want to use bone-in meat or
something needing longer cooking,
such as lamb, just add more water
and let simmer.

SRI LANKAN-STYLE COCONUT DHAL

SERVES 2–3 AS A MAIN OR 4–6 AS A SIDE WITH OTHER DISHES
PREP TIME: 15 MINS • COOK TIME: 28 MINS
WF • GF • DF • V • Ve • NF • SoF • SUITABLE FOR FREEZING

10½ ounces **split red lentils**

2 cups **cold water**, or more as needed

½ teaspoon **ground turmeric**

4 tablespoons **neutral cooking oil**

1 teaspoon **mustard seeds**

½ teaspoon **cumin seeds**

a generous pinch of **fenugreek seeds**

6 **curry leaves**

1 small **onion**, finely sliced

1 medium **green chili pepper**, finely
    chopped

2 cloves of **garlic**, crushed

6 tablespoons **coconut cream**

salt and **freshly ground black pepper**

This is something you'll often find—albeit made in lots of different ways—in a Sri Lankan home-cooked meal. This is our version.

Rinse the red lentils a couple of times in cold water and drain. Place the lentils in a large saucepan with a lid, cover with the cold water, add the turmeric, and bring to a simmer. Use a slotted spoon to skim off any scum that rises to the surface. Reduce the heat to low and cook for 15–20 minutes, stirring every now and then and topping up with water if necessary, until the lentils are tender and just beginning to collapse.

Meanwhile, heat the oil in a small skillet set over a medium heat. Add the mustard seeds and, when they start to pop, add the cumin seeds, fenugreek seeds, and curry leaves. Let the seeds toast for 1 minute or so, then add the onion. Cook for 8–10 minutes, stirring very frequently, until the onion begins to brown. Add the chili pepper, the garlic, and a pinch of salt (to help the onions release their juices and stop the garlic from burning), and cook for 3 minutes. Remove from the heat.

Spoon the coconut cream into the cooked lentils and cook for 3 minutes, stirring. Remove from the heat and tip the contents of the onion pan into the lentil dhal. Mix well, then taste for salt and season generously.

Serve immediately, with rice, breads, and something yogurt-y, or as part of a spread of curries.

≡ TIP ≡

If you leave out the chili pepper and cut back on the salt, this is an excellent meal for small kids. Rebecca freezes portions of it in reusable baking cups —perfect portions for toddlers.

LEMONGRASS COCONUT EGGPLANT CURRY

SERVES 4
PREP TIME: 15 MINS • COOK TIME: 30 MINS
WF • GF • DF • V • Ve • SoF

4 medium **eggplants**, stem ends trimmed, halved crossways, then cut into ¾-inch wedges

3 tablespoons **neutral cooking oil**

2½ cups **coconut milk**

2 sticks of **lemongrass**, bruised with a rolling pin until almost flat

4 **scallions**, roughly chopped

2 cloves of **garlic**, crushed

8 **lime leaves**, roughly torn

1 teaspoon **ground turmeric**

1 teaspoon **ground cumin**

a generous pinch of **crushed pepper flakes** (optional)

2 ounces **roasted unsalted peanuts**, chopped

finely grated zest of ½ **lime** (unwaxed)

salt

This simple curry packs way more punch than its quick-and-easy prep suggests.

Heat the oven to 400°F.

Put the wedges of eggplant and the oil into a roasting pan and use your hands to toss it all together, making sure each piece is lightly coated in the oil. Roast for 20 minutes, turning the wedges halfway through.

Meanwhile, in a large bowl, combine the coconut milk, lemongrass, scallions, garlic, lime leaves, turmeric, cumin, crushed red pepper, if using, and a good pinch of salt. Mix well.

Remove the eggplant pan from the oven and pour the coconut mixture over the wedges, turning each one to ensure they are all coated in the coconut curry. Return to the oven for a further 10 minutes.

Tip the peanuts onto a baking tray, and put them in the oven for the last 7 minutes of the curry's cooking time.

Remove both pan and tray from the oven and set the eggplant curry aside, while you tip the nuts into a mortar and pestle and lightly pummel. Add the lime zest and a small pinch of salt.

Remove and discard the lime leaves and lemongrass from the eggplant curry, then serve the curry sprinkled with the peanut and lime zest topping.

SOUTH INDIAN-STYLE FISH CURRY

SERVES 4

PREP TIME: 15 MINS • COOK TIME: 35 MINS

WF • GF • DF • NF • SoF (check flatbreads)

1 tablespoon **neutral cooking oil**

1 teaspoon **mustard seeds**

6 **curry leaves**

1 **onion**, finely sliced

¼ teaspoon **cumin seeds**

4 **cloves**

4 **green cardamom pods**

2 cloves of **garlic**

1-inch piece of **ginger**, peeled and grated

2 **green chili peppers**, deseeded and finely chopped

4 ounces (about 1 large) **tomato**, deseeded and finely chopped

1 teaspoon **ground turmeric**

¼–½ teaspoon **chili powder**

1¾ cups **coconut milk**

14 ounces **firm white fish** (**salmon** or **trout**, or a mixture), cut into large chunks

10 ounces **zucchini**, halved and sliced into ¼-inch strips

12–16 large **raw shrimp**, depending on size

a pinch of **salt** and **freshly ground black pepper**

freshly squeezed lemon or **lime juice**, to taste

rice or **Indian flatbreads** (pages 198–201 and 205–206), to serve

This is based on a famous dish called meen moilee. To make it vegan, just add more vegetables along with the zucchini—green beans, peas, sugar snap peas, sliced bell peppers, cooked squash or sweet potato. Shellfish also work brilliantly—just cook for 3–4 minutes in the broth with the lid on.

Heat the oil in a large saucepan with a lid, set over a medium heat. When hot, add the mustard seeds and curry leaves and, when the seeds start to pop, add the onion, salt, cumin seeds, cloves, and cardamom pods. Cook for 6–8 minutes, stirring, until the onions are soft but not brown. Add the garlic, ginger, chili peppers, tomato, turmeric, and chili powder, and cook for a further 5–8 minutes, until the tomato has broken down and the mixture is fragrant, with a glossy, oily sheen.

Reduce the heat to low, add about one-quarter of the coconut milk, and bring to a boil, then add the rest of the coconut milk. Increase the heat to medium and bring to a simmer. Season with some black pepper, then taste and add more chili powder if you'd like more heat.

Add the fish and zucchini to the pan, gently pressing them into the broth. Cover with a lid and cook for 4 minutes, then remove the lid and add the shrimp, pressing them into the broth, but being careful not to break up the fish too much. Cover again and cook for a final 2 minutes. When you remove the lid, the fish should be cooked through and the shrimp pink throughout.

Remove from the heat. Taste and add a squeeze of lemon or lime juice, if needed, then serve immediately with rice or Indian flatbreads.

WEST AFRICAN-STYLE PEANUT CURRY

SERVES 4
PREP TIME: 20 MINS • COOK TIME: 55 MINS
WF • GF • DF • V • Ve • SoF

1 tablespoon **neutral cooking oil**

2 **onions**, finely diced

2 cloves of **garlic**, crushed

¾-inch piece of **ginger**, peeled and grated

½ **red bell pepper**, deseeded and diced

2 teaspoons **tomato paste**

½ teaspoon **ground coriander**

½ teaspoon **ground cumin**

½ teaspoon **ground turmeric**

½–1 teaspoon **cayenne pepper**

14 ounces **canned diced tomatoes**, undrained

1¾ cups **hot water**

2 ounces **creamy peanut butter** (unsweetened)

1¼ pounds (2 medium) **sweet potatoes**, peeled and diced

14 ounces **canned chickpeas**, drained

5 ounces **kale**, or any sweet, soft-leaved **green cabbage**, stems and ribs removed, finely shredded

2 ounces **okra**, trimmed and cut into ½-inch rounds (optional)

salt and **freshly ground black pepper**

1 **red chili pepper**, deseeded and finely sliced, to serve

a handful of **toasted unsalted peanuts**, chopped, to serve

There are so many of our favorite LEON ingredients in this, that it makes us hum tunes from **The Sound of Music***: kale, sweet potato, chickpeas, chilies and earthy, warming spices.*

Heat the oil in a large heavy saucepan over a medium heat. Add the onion and sauté gently for about 8 minutes, until soft. Add the garlic, ginger, and bell pepper and cook for 3–4 minutes, until fragrant. Add the tomato paste and all the ground spices (use only ½ teaspoon cayenne pepper to begin with) and cook for 2 minutes, stirring all the time, until fragrant.

Add the tomatoes and their juice, the water (just fill the tomato can), peanut butter, and sweet potatoes. Stir well, then bring to a simmer. Partly cover with a lid, reduce the heat, and gently cook until the sweet potatoes are tender, about 20–25 minutes.

Add the drained chickpeas to the pan and simmer for another 5–10 minutes, then add the kale and okra, if using. Stir well, then simmer for a further 5 minutes, just until the kale is done. Remove from the heat and taste for salt and pepper. You can even add a pinch more cayenne, if you like.

Serve with the red chili pepper slices and chopped peanuts, sprinkled on top.

≡ TIP ≡

If you only have crunchy peanut butter, no worries—you will just end up with a nuttier texture.

SPEEDY

SKINNY PARCEL-BAKED SALMON & EGGPLANT CURRY

SERVES 2
PREP TIME: 15 MINS • COOK TIME: 25 MINS
WF • GF • DF • NF • SoF

1 teaspoon **fennel seeds**

4 **green cardamom pods**

1 tablespoon **neutral cooking oil**

1 teaspoon peeled and finely grated **ginger**

1 clove of **garlic**, crushed

2 tablespoons (about 1) finely grated **shallot**

1 teaspoon **ground coriander**

½ teaspoon **ground cumin**

½ teaspoon **ground turmeric**

1 teaspoon **tamarind paste** or
  concentrate (optional)

1 tablespoon **freshly squeezed lime juice**

3 tablespoons **coconut milk**

a pinch of **sugar**

2 skinless **salmon fillets** (or any fish fillets)

10 ounces **zucchini**, cut into ¼-inch slices
  on an angle

salt and **freshly ground black pepper**

steamed **wild and basmati rice**, to serve

lemon wedges, to serve

≡ TIP ≡

Switch the zucchini for any other crisp green veg—beans, asparagus, or a mixture. Make it more of a one-pot dish by adding sliced cooked new potatoes to the parcel.

This is a super-light and low-fat curry, which is also very simple to make.

Place the fennel seeds and cardamom pods in a mortar and pestle (or use a rolling pin) and lightly bash, just to bruise and release their flavor. Tip into a large bowl with the oil, ginger, garlic, shallot, ground coriander, cumin, turmeric, and tamarind concentrate, if using. Stir in the lime juice, coconut milk, sugar, a good pinch of salt, and some freshly ground black pepper. Mix to form a paste. Add the salmon fillets and zucchini slices to the bowl, mix well, and use your hands to rub the paste into each piece.

Heat the oven to 350°F.

Tear off a long sheet of parchment paper or foil and lay it on top of a baking sheet so that one of the shorter sides is closest to you. Arrange the zucchini slices in a rough layer in the center of the paper or foil, about 2 slices thick. Top with the salmon, then scrape any remaining paste from the bowl and dot it on top. Bring the long sides of the paper or foil together over the fish and fold down, then fold the short ends together several times, enclosing the fish tightly and completely so that the steam cannot escape.

Bake for 25 minutes. When you unwrap the parcel, the zucchini should be just tender and the fish should be cooked through.

Serve with wild and basmati rice and lemon wedges.

CORNERSHOP CURRY

SERVES 4
PREP TIME: 10 MINS • COOK TIME: 26 MINS
WF • GF • DF • NF • SoF (check curry paste and flatbreads)

1 tablespoon **neutral cooking oil**

2 **onions**, finely diced

5 tablespoons **Indian-style curry paste from a jar** (we like fiery Madras)

10 ounces **canned diced tomatoes**, undrained

14 ounces **canned green beans**, drained

13 ounces **canned mackerel fillets** (ideally in oil), drained

ready-made flatbreads or **microwave rice**, to serve

TIP

Mix and match with other cans from your local store—use sardines, or go veggie and use cooked lentils, chickpeas, or cannellini beans; experiment with other canned veg—peas, potatoes, or carrots.

It's cold. It's ages until payday. You're knackered… So make this! It will warm you up and soothe your soul. And, we promise, it's all made with things you can find in the shop at the end of the road. (Rebecca invented this curry when in need of something better than beans on toast but almost as quick, on a day filled with deadlines. She has also been known to fry spice paste from a jar and then mix it with a tin of lentil soup—cheat's dhal!)

Heat the oil in a large heavy saucepan set over a medium heat. Add the onions and sauté gently for about 8 minutes, until soft. Add the curry paste and fry, stirring, for about 3 minutes. Add ¼ cup of water and mix well, then simmer for a few minutes until most of the water has evaporated and the paste has a glossy, oily sheen.

Add the tomatoes with a spoon, leaving most of the juice behind. Reduce the heat to low, stir well, and break up any lumps with the back of the spoon, then simmer for 8–10 minutes, or until the tomatoes have melted into the sauce.

Add the beans and the mackerel, plus another ¼–½ cup water, if the curry looks at all dry. Stir gently, being careful not to break up the fish too much, then cover with a lid. Increase the heat to medium, bring to a simmer, and cook for 3–4 minutes, until everything is heated through.

Serve with ready-made flatbreads (or even pita bread), or microwaved rice.

≡ TIP ≡

You can do this with
skin-on fillets of any fish,
just decrease the fish's initial
cooking time to 7–8 minutes,
depending on how large the
fillets are.

BAKED MACKEREL CURRY

SERVES 4
PREP TIME: 20 MINS • COOK TIME: 40 MINS
WF • GF • DF • NF • SoF

1½ pounds **new** or **baby potatoes**, halved

½ head **fennel**, finely sliced

1 large **onion**, finely sliced

1 pound **cherry tomatoes**, halved

1½ tablespoons **neutral cooking oil**

4 small whole **mackerel**, cleaned and gutted

salt, to taste

FOR THE SPICE PASTE:

2 teaspoons **ground turmeric**

1½-inch piece of **ginger**, peeled and grated

3 cloves of **garlic**, crushed

1 tablespoon **mustard seeds**

1 tablespoon **fennel seeds**

¼ teaspoon **salt**

2 teaspoons **coriander seeds**

2 teaspoons **cumin seeds**

a generous grinding of **black pepper**

1 **red chili pepper** (deseeded or not, to taste), finely chopped

FOR THE GREENS:

12 ounces **chard** or **spinach**, stems removed

2 teaspoons **neutral cooking oil**

1 teaspoon **black mustard seeds**

1 clove of **garlic**, crushed

a pinch of **salt**

We love a baked curry—they are so easy. We also love heart-healthy mackerel, so we invented this.

Heat the oven to 400°F.

Bring a large saucepan of salted water to a boil, then parboil the potatoes for 9 minutes. Drain.

Tip the potatoes into a large roasting pan (or two smaller ones), and add the fennel, onion, cherry tomatoes, and 1 tablespoon of the oil. Toss until everything is coated in the oil, then roast in the oven for 15 minutes.

Meanwhile, grind the spice paste ingredients to a paste in a mortar and pestle.

Remove the pan from the oven, add two-thirds of the spice paste to the vegetables, and toss together thoroughly. Rub the mackerel, inside and out, with the remaining third of the spice paste, drizzle with the remaining ½ tablespoon of oil, and rest the fish on top of the vegetables. Sprinkle with a pinch of salt and return to the oven for a further 10 minutes.

Remove the pan from the oven, add about ¼ cup water, and return to the oven for a final 5 minutes.

Meanwhile, make the greens. Wash the chard or spinach and drain in a colander, but do not dry. Heat the oil in a wide skillet over a medium heat. When hot, add the mustard seeds and, as soon as they begin to pop, add the garlic and salt and cook for 1 minute, stirring. Add the freshly washed greens and cook for 3–4 minutes, stirring, until wilted.

Serve the fish with the pan-baked curry, with the greens on the side.

CHANA MASALA

SERVES 2 AS A MAIN OR 4 AS A SIDE

PREP TIME: 15 MINS • COOK TIME: 35 MINS

WF • GF • DF • V • VE • NF • SoF • SUITABLE FOR FREEZING

1 tablespoon **neutral cooking oil**

1 **onion**, finely sliced

2 teaspoons **mustard seeds**

1½ teaspoons **cumin seeds**

1-inch piece of **ginger,** peeled and grated

2 cloves of **garlic**, crushed

10 **curry leaves**

1 teaspoon **ground coriander**

1 teaspoon **garam masala**

1 tablespoon finely chopped **green chili pepper** (or more for a hotter curry)

7 ounces **diced tomatoes** (fresh and skinned, or canned)

14 ounces **canned chickpeas**, undrained (canned kala chana, brown chickpeas, are ideal)

salt, to taste

squeeze of **lemon juice**, to serve

a generous handful of **fresh cilantro**, to garnish (optional)

≡ TIP ≡

If you happen to have some sour green mango powder (amchoor/amchur) lying around, then a pinch works well here, as does a spoonful of tamarind concentrate or paste.

Chickpeas have always been our friends at LEON. We have had them on the menu, in the form of hummus, every day since we opened our first LEON on Carnaby Street in 2004. This is easy, vegan and scrumptious.

Heat the oil in a large saucepan with a lid over a medium heat. When hot, add the onion and cook for about 8 minutes, stirring often, until beginning to brown. Add the mustard and cumin seeds and cook for a minute or so, until the mustard seeds begin to pop, then add the ginger, garlic, curry leaves, ground coriander, garam masala, and chili pepper. Cook for 5 minutes, stirring, so that the garlic and ginger don't stick and burn.

Finally, add the diced tomatoes and the chickpeas, along with the water from the can. Stir well to combine, then reduce the heat to low, cover with a lid, and simmer gently for about 15 minutes. Check every now and then to make sure the pan isn't drying out, and add a splash of water if needed.

Taste and decide if you want to add any salt (some brands of chickpeas are rather salty). Remove from the heat and, just before serving, add a squeeze of lemon juice and some fresh cilantro leaves.

TOFU PHAD PHRIK KHING

SERVES 4
PREP TIME: 20 MINS • COOK TIME: 20 MINS
WF • GF • DF • V • VE • NF • SoF

1 pound **extra-firm tofu,** cut into
¾ x ¾- inch squares, about ½ inch thick

2–4 tablespoons **neutral cooking oil**

3 tablespoons good-quality **Thai red
curry paste** (choose a vegan brand if
necessary, or use the recipe on page 43,
omitting the fish sauce)

7 ounces **Chinese long beans,** cut into
1-inch pieces

7 ounces **Asian greens** (we like choy sum),
sliced into 1-inch strips

3 ounces **broccoli,** cut into bite-size
pieces

4 **lime leaves,** stems removed, leaves
sliced into paper-thin strips

2–3 tablespoons **water**

freshly squeezed lime juice

salt

steamed jasmine rice, to serve

≡ TIP ≡

Non-vegans may like to splash
in a little fish sauce, which is a
traditional Thai ingredient.

*This dry Thai curry is usually made just with long green beans, but we
like to add extra greenery for goodness and flavor. If you like your curries
hot, taste the curry paste first—you may want to add extra fresh or dried
red chilies.*

Line a large plate or cutting board with 2 sheets of paper towel and arrange the tofu
in a single layer on top. Cover with more paper towel and use your hands or another
board to gently press out as much liquid as you can—this will result in crisper tofu
when cooked.

Heat 2 tablespoons of the oil in a large skillet or wok set over a medium heat.
Working in batches if necessary and adding more oil as needed, fry the tofu until
golden on both sides, about 4 minutes per side. Don't try to move the tofu too
soon—it will stick at first and then gradually release from the pan as it cooks. Set
the cooked tofu aside and keep warm.

If the pan looks dry, add another tablespoon of oil, then add the curry paste, and
cook, stirring, for 1 minute. Add the beans, greens, broccoli, and lime leaves, plus
1 tablespoon of water, and sauté for 3 minutes, moving everything around constantly
and adding more of the water if the pan is very dry.

Remove from the heat, gently stir in the hot tofu, and coat in the sauce. Squeeze over
a little lime juice, then taste and add salt as needed (how much, if any, will depend on
the type of curry paste you used). Serve alongside a mound of jasmine rice.

QUICKEST CURRY EVER

2 tablespoons **neutral cooking oil**

1 small **onion**, finely sliced

1 teaspoon **paprika**

½ teaspoon **chili powder**

¼ teaspoon **ground turmeric**

½ teaspoon **ground cumin**

¼ teaspoon **ground coriander**

2 teaspoons **tomato paste**

1 medium **tomato**, deseeded, cored, and finely diced

1-inch piece of **ginger**, peeled and finely grated

2 cloves of **garlic**, crushed

5 ounces **carrot**, peeled and cut into thin slivers

1 **bell pepper**, deseeded and finely sliced

7 ounces **cauliflower**, broken into very small florets

5 ounces **Chinese long beans**, finely sliced on an angle

1 **green chili pepper**, finely chopped

3 tablespoons **water**

salt and **freshly ground black pepper**

Naan (see page 198), to serve

a handful of **fresh cilantro**, to garnish

Vegetable jalfrezi is a fabulous, fairly fiery vegan main course, or a super-quick spicy side.

Heat the oil in a large skillet or wok with a lid, set over a medium-high heat. When hot, add the onion and cook for 5 minutes, until softened.

Meanwhile, mix all the ground spices together in a bowl.

Add the tomato paste to the pan, stir to coat the onions, and cook for about 2 minutes. Add all the vegetables and the mixed spices and stir-fry for 3–4 minutes—we like the vegetables to have a lot of bite. Add some salt and pepper and the water, mix well, and cover with the lid. Let steam for a further 3 minutes, until the vegetables are just tender but still have a crisp bite.

Serve with naan and sprinkled with the fresh cilantro.

═ **TIP** ═

This is a great way of using up small quantities of stray vegetables in the fridge—a lonely carrot or a solitary bell pepper. Use this as a guide and add anything from mushrooms to zucchini to frozen peas.

SMOKY CURRY-SPICED LAMB CHOPS

SERVES 4
PREP TIME: 10 MINS, PLUS OPTIONAL 4 HOURS MARINATING • COOK TIME: 6 MINS
WF • GF • NF • SoF

2 cloves of **garlic**, crushed

1-inch piece of **ginger**, peeled and finely grated

1 teaspoon **ground cumin**

1 teaspoon **ground coriander**

½ teaspoon **chili powder**

1 teaspoon **sweet smoked paprika**

1 tablespoon **whole-milk plain yogurt**

1 teaspoon **freshly squeezed lemon** or **lime juice**

a really generous pinch of **salt** and some **freshly ground black pepper**

4–8 (depending on their size and your appetite) thick **lamb chops**

TO SERVE:
Choose one or two of the following:

Dhal (pages 26, 79, and 135)

Raita (pages 163–164)

Tamarind Yogurt (page 165)

Kachumber Salad (page 192)

Koshambari Salad (page 191)

rice or **Indian flatbreads** (pages 198–201 and 205–206)

For an altogether more interesting take on meat-and-two-veg, serve these chops with Sag Paneer (page 60), Dhal (pages 26, 79 and 135) and some Bombay Potatoes (page 187).

In a large bowl, mix together all the ingredients, except the chops, until well combined. Add the chops and rub the marinade all over the meat, working it in with your fingers. If possible, leave to marinate for 4 hours or so, but you can cook immediately, if you want.

Turn on the broiler and wait for it to get really hot.

Shake or scrape any excess marinade from the chops—you want a little coating the meat, but not so much that the meat is wet, as it won't brown. Cook the chops under the broiler for 2–3 minutes per side, or until the marinade is sizzling and the edges of the fat are beginning to brown, and the meat is cooked to your liking—we like it pink. (Exactly how long depends on the power of your broiler and the thickness of the chops.)

Serve with one or two of the suggested accompaniments.

⹀ TIP ⹀

We cook this under the broiler as the marinade is less likely to burn, but feel free to cook these in a very hot griddle pan, or on the BBQ, where you'll get more tasty charred bits.

CURRY-SPICED TOFU

SERVES 4
PREP TIME: 15 MINS, PLUS OPTIONAL 10–30 MINS MARINATING • COOK TIME: 30 MINS
WF • GF • DF • V • VE • NF

14 ounces **extra-firm tofu**, cut into
 ¾–1-inch slices, about ½ inch thick

1 clove of **garlic**, crushed

1 teaspoon **peeled and finely grated
 ginger**

½ teaspoon **ground cumin**

¼ teaspoon **ground coriander**

¼ teaspoon **ground turmeric**

a pinch of **ground cinnamon**

a pinch of **chili powder** (optional)

1 teaspoon **soy sauce**

1 teaspoon **neutral cooking oil**, plus extra
 for greasing

a pinch of **salt** and **freshly ground
 black pepper**

These little nuggets of tofu work brilliantly on top of vegetarian curries.

Line a plate or cutting board with 2 sheets of parchment paper and arrange the tofu in a single layer on top. Cover with more parchment paper and use your hands or another board or plate to gently press out as much liquid as you can—this will result in crisper tofu when cooked.

Mix together the remaining ingredients to form a paste. Spread this on the top and bottom of each slice of tofu. If you have time, leave to marinate for 10–30 minutes, but you can cook immediately, if wished.

When ready to cook, heat the oven to 400°F. Line a baking sheet with parchment paper and brush it with a little oil.

Place the tofu on the baking sheet and bake for 30 minutes, turning once halfway through, until golden brown. Serve immediately.

≡ TIP ≡

Mustard oil adds a peppery, earthy note to this, so you could drizzle over a little just before serving.

THAI-SPICED TOFU

SERVES 4

PREP TIME: 10 MINS, PLUS OPTIONAL 10–30 MINS MARINATING • COOK TIME: 8 MINS

WF • GF • DF • V • VE (if made without fish sauce; also check curry and chili paste ingredients) • NF

14 ounces **extra-firm tofu**, cut into
  ¾–1-inch slices, about ½ inch thick
2 tablespoons good-quality **Thai red
  curry paste** (choose a vegan brand if
  necessary, or use the recipe on page 43,
  omitting the fish sauce)
neutral cooking oil
salt, to taste

TO DRESS:
freshly squeezed lime juice
fish sauce
Thai Sriracha hot sauce
Thai chili paste (nam prik pao; check for
  shrimp paste, if vegan or vegetarian)
chili oil
sesame oil

This is a great way to add extra protein to a vegan curry, as well as adding flavor to notoriously bland tofu. Use it to top any Thai curry or in a Thai main dish, in place of meat or fish.

Line a plate or cutting board with 2 sheets of paper towel and arrange the tofu in a single layer on top. Cover with more paper towel and use your hands or another board or plate to gently press out as much liquid as you can—this will result in crisper tofu when cooked.

Use your hands to gently rub the Thai red curry paste over and into each slice of tofu. If you have time, leave to marinate for 10–30 minutes, but you can cook immediately, if wished.

Heat a ½-inch depth of oil in a nonstick skillet set over a medium-low heat. When hot, slide in the tofu slices (work in batches if necessary) and cook, fairly gently, for about 4 minutes on each side, until the tofu is golden and beginning to crisp up and the curry paste is dark red, but not scorched. Repeat until all the slices have been cooked, keeping the cooked slices warm.

Season with a little salt and dress with one or two of the suggested options, to fit whatever you are serving it with.

= TIP =

Be sure your brand of tofu is firm—the silky, wobbly kind won't work here.

SRI LANKAN-STYLE GREEN BEAN & ZUCCHINI CURRY

SERVES 4

PREP TIME: 15 MINS • COOK TIME: 20 MINS

WF • GF • DF • V • VE • NF • SoF

7 ounces **shallots**, finely sliced

2 teaspoons **finely chopped green chili pepper**

1¼ pounds **zucchini**, sliced into ¼-inch pieces

10 ounces **Chinese long beans**, trimmed

1 teaspoon **ground turmeric**

a generous pinch of **fenugreek seeds**

10 **curry leaves**

1¼ cups **coconut milk**

¼–½ teaspoon **salt**, or to taste

¼ teaspoon **chili powder**, or to taste

rice or **Indian flatbreads** (pages 198–201 and 205–206), to serve

FOR THE ROASTED CURRY POWDER GARNISH:

½ teaspoon **uncooked rice**

¼ teaspoon each **black mustard**, **coriander**, **cumin**, and **fennel seeds**

a pinch of **fenugreek seeds**

¼ teaspoon **crushed red pepper**

2 **cloves**

seeds from 3 **green cardamom pods**

4 **curry leaves**

¼ teaspoon **ground turmeric**

This simple pale-yellow curry is often served very hot and spicy in Sri Lanka, so feel free to ramp up the chili content for a more authentic version. The roasted Sri Lankan curry powder isn't essential, but lasts well if sealed in a jar.

First make the roasted curry powder garnish, if using: heat a dry skillet over a medium heat. When hot, add the rice and mustards seeds and, when the seeds start to crackle, add all the other ingredients, except the turmeric. Cook, stirring constantly, for 3–5 minutes, until well toasted—the aim is to get the mixture off the heat just before the spices burn. Remove from the heat and stir the turmeric into the pan, then tip everything out into a mortar and pestle and grind to a powder. Set aside.

Place all the ingredients for the curry, except the chili powder, into a large saucepan with a lid. Stir well to ensure the spices are mixed into the coconut milk and the zucchini is well coated, and press the vegetables down into the liquid. Place the pan over a low heat, cover, and slowly bring to a simmer (don't rush, as the coconut milk may separate). Simmer gently for 10 minutes, stirring once or twice, until the zucchini is just tender and the beans still have some bite (check after 6 minutes or so, to ensure the vegetables aren't cooking too fast). Taste to check salt levels, and add the chili powder.

Serve in wide bowls, sprinkled with a pinch of the roasted curry powder, if using, with flatbreads or rice.

TIP

Although delish on its own, Sri Lankans often eat a range of curry dishes and sides together, so you could serve this with Dhal (pages 26, 79, and 135) and a meat or fish curry, as well.

TIP

Any mixture of
seafood, including
shellfish, will work here—
just cook, lid on, for 3–4
minutes, until the shells
pop open.

BURMESE-STYLE FISH, SHRIMP, & TOMATO CURRY

SERVES 2

PREP TIME: 20 MINS • COOK TIME: 20 MINS

WF • GF • DF • NF • SoF

2 teaspoons **ground turmeric**

¼–½ teaspoon **cayenne pepper**

1 tablespoon **fish sauce**, or more to taste

14 ounces **firm white fish** or **salmon**, cut into 1-inch chunks

2 **onions**, roughly diced

3 cloves of **garlic**, roughly chopped

1½-inch piece of **ginger**, peeled and roughly chopped

½–1 medium **red chili pepper** (deseeded to taste), roughly chopped

2 tablespoons **neutral cooking oil**

1 pound **fresh tomatoes**, blitzed until smooth in a food processor (or 1 pound **canned diced tomatoes**)

2 teaspoons **sweet paprika**

10 ounces **raw shrimp**, peeled (deveined if you prefer)

a generous pinch of **crushed red pepper** (optional)

1 tablespoon **freshly squeezed lime juice**, plus 4 **lime wedges**

a large handful of **fresh cilantro**, roughly chopped

steamed rice, to serve

A simple—but brilliantly tasty—curry, this is a spin on a recipe Rebecca found in the wonderful book **Share***, by Alison Oakervee, a collection of uplifting recipes from war-torn countries, with the non-profit organization Women for Women International.*

In a large bowl, mix the turmeric, cayenne, and fish sauce to a paste, add the fish, and toss to thoroughly coat in the mixture. Cover and set aside.

In a small blender, blitz the onions, garlic, ginger, and chili pepper to a coarse purée, scraping down the sides with a spatula. (Alternatively, use a mortar and pestle.)

Heat the oil in a large deep saucepan with a lid over a medium heat. When hot, add the onion mixture and cook for about 10 minutes, stirring frequently, until translucent and beginning to brown. Add the tomatoes and bring to a simmer. Stir in the paprika, reduce the heat to low, and simmer for 5 minutes, or until the raw flavor of the tomatoes disappears—taste to be sure. (If using canned tomatoes and the sauce seems dry, add a little water to the pan and bring back to a simmer.) Add the fish and marinade, cover, and cook for 3 minutes, then gently stir and taste. Add more fish sauce for saltiness, or the crushed red pepper for more heat.

Next, push the shrimp into the curry. Cook for 1–2 minutes, until pink. Remove from the heat, and add the lime juice and most of the chopped cilantro. Stir once, being careful not to break up the fish too much.

Serve with steamed rice, sprinkled with the remaining cilantro and with lime wedges to squeeze over.

RAJMA

SERVES 2 AS A MAIN OR 4 WITH OTHER DISHES
PREP TIME: 10 MINS • COOK TIME: 28 MINS
WF • GF • V • VE • DF (if using vegan ghee) **• NF • SoF • SUITABLE FOR FREEZING**

1 tablespoon **neutral cooking oil**

1 **onion**, finely chopped

2 cloves of **garlic**, crushed

1-inch piece of **ginger**, peeled and grated

1 medium **green chili pepper**, deseeded and finely chopped

1½ tablespoons **tomato paste**

6 **green cardamom pods**

¼ teaspoon **ground cinnamon**

¼ teaspoon **ground cumin**

½ teaspoon **ground coriander**

a pinch of **chili powder** (or less, to taste)

½ teaspoon **garam masala**

14 ounces **canned kidney beans in water**, undrained

1 **bay leaf**

a pinch of **sugar**

a knob of **butter** or **ghee** (optional but magical) (ghee can be vegan)

a handful of **fresh cilantro**

salt and **freshly ground black pepper**

steamed rice or **Naan** (see page 198), to serve

This incredibly restorative kidney bean curry is usually served with rice but we often serve it with some fluffy naan to create a northern Indian equivalent of beans on toast.

Heat the oil in a medium saucepan over a medium heat. Add the onion and cook for about 8 minutes, stirring often, until just beginning to brown.

Reduce the heat to low, add the garlic, ginger, and chili pepper, and cook for 2 minutes, stirring. Stir in the tomato paste and cook for 3 minutes, stirring to prevent the mixture from sticking. Add all the spices and continue to stir for 1 minute (don't let the mixture stick and burn or the spices will become bitter). Add the kidney beans, along with the water from the can, bay leaf, sugar, and some salt and pepper. Fill the can one-third full with water, then pour that into the pan, too. Increase the heat and bring to a boil, then reduce the heat and simmer for 15 minutes, stirring now and then.

Remove from the heat and stir through the knob of butter or ghee, if using, and taste for salt and pepper. Remove and discard the bay leaf and cardamom pods, if you can find them, then stir through the cilantro leaves.

Serve with steamed rice or warm naan.

For a posh dinner party or restaurant-style touch, add 3 tablespoons of cream just before serving.

FISH BHUNA

SERVES 4

PREP TIME: 18 MINS • COOK TIME: 35 MINS, PLUS 5 MINS STANDING

WF • GF • DF • NF • SoF

1 tablespoon **neutral cooking oil**

1 **onion**, finely sliced

2 cloves of **garlic**, crushed

1-inch piece of **ginger**, peeled and finely grated

6 **green cardamom pods**, bruised

¼ teaspoon **fennel seeds**

¼ teaspoon **ground turmeric**

¼ teaspoon **chili powder**

½ teaspoon **garam masala**

½ teaspoon **ground coriander**

½ cup **water**, plus extra as needed

1 tablespoon **tomato paste**

2 medium **tomatoes**, deseeded, cored, and very finely chopped

4 fillets of any **firm white fish**, each cut into 2 or 3 large pieces

a pinch of **salt**

lemon wedges, to serve

Hold your nerve when cooking the spices for this—they need some intense pan-roasting (although, don't burn 'em). The sauce should be thick enough to coat the fish, when cooked.

Heat the oil in a large saucepan with a lid, set over a medium heat. Add the onions and cook for about 8–10 minutes, stirring, until they begin to brown. Add the garlic and ginger and sizzle for 30 seconds. Mix all the spices together with a pinch of salt, then add to the pan and cook for 1½ minutes, until fragrant and almost—but not quite—burning.

Add the water and simmer until the water is almost entirely evaporated, about 10 minutes, leaving a thick paste with an oily sheen. Add the tomato paste and fresh tomatoes to the pan and cook gently until the tomatoes have softened, about 6–8 minutes. Add the fish to the pan, along with 1 or 2 tablespoons of water—just enough to stop everything sticking, but not so much that the sauce becomes at all watery. Reduce the heat to low, cover, and let the fish part-fry, part-steam in the pan for about 5 minutes.

Remove from the heat, uncover, very gently stir once, and leave to stand for 5 minutes before serving.

≡ TIP ≡

This also works with boneless chicken, cut into strips, but you will need to increase the cooking time a little.

GYM BUNNY CURRY

SERVES 4
PREP TIME: 15 MINS • COOK TIME: 45 MINS
DF • V WF • **GF** (if served with rice) • **NF** • **SoF** (if using NF or SoF yogurt)

4 **eggs**

1 tablespoon **neutral cooking oil**

4 **curry leaves**, torn

½ teaspoon **cumin seeds**

1 **onion**, finely diced

1-inch piece of **ginger**, peeled and finely grated

1 clove of **garlic**, crushed

1 **red chili pepper**, finely chopped

6 **green cardamom pods**

1 teaspoon **ground turmeric**

1 teaspoon **ground coriander**

14 ounces **canned diced tomatoes**, undrained

5 tablespoons **coconut milk (or whole-milk plain yogurt** or **nondairy yogurt)**

a handful of **fresh cilantro**, to serve

rice or **Indian flatbreads** (pages 198–201 and 205–206), to serve

≡ TIP ≡

This is a good lunchbox curry—cook the eggs in the morning, then take to work in their shells. Peel and warm everything up together.

A high-protein curry, perfect post workout. No bunnies involved.

Place the eggs in a deep saucepan with a lid and cover with water by about ¾ inch. Set over a high heat and bring to a rolling boil, then remove from the heat, cover with a lid, and let stand for 8 minutes. Use tongs to remove the eggs from the pan, then cool under cold running water. Peel and set aside.

Heat the oil in a large saucepan set over a medium heat. Add the curry leaves and cumin seeds and sizzle for 2 minutes, then add the onion and cook for about 8 minutes, stirring, until translucent. Add the ginger, garlic, chili pepper, cardamom, turmeric, and ground coriander, and cook, stirring, for about 5 minutes, or until it forms an oily-looking paste and smells delicious. Add the tomatoes and ½ cup water, then stir well, scraping any paste up from the bottom of the pan, and bring to a simmer.

Reduce the heat to low and cook for up to 30 minutes, squashing any lumps of tomato with the back of a spoon, until it is thick, tart, and spicy, and the raw flavor of the tomatoes has completely disappeared (add a splash of water if the pan gets too dry).

Remove from the heat and stir in the coconut milk and half the cilantro. Cut the eggs in half and place in the hot curry, to warm through. Serve with the rest of the cilantro sprinkled on top, with rice or Indian flatbreads.

DORO ALICHA TIBS

SERVES 4
PREP TIME: 20 MINS • COOK TIME: 30 MINS
WF • GF • NF • SoF

2 tablespoons **neutral cooking oil**

1 large **onion**, diced

¾-inch piece of **ginger**, peeled and grated

2 cloves of **garlic**, crushed

1 tablespoon **paprika**

a generous pinch of **ground cardamom**

a generous pinch of **ground cinnamon**

1¼ pounds **chicken breast** and boneless **thighs**, chopped into small pieces

a generous pinch of **salt**

1 **plum tomato**, diced

green chili peppers, deseeded and thinly sliced, to garnish

rice and **salad**, **cooked green beans** or **cabbage**, to serve

Every Friday, the team at the LEON support office in London descends on a nearby street food stall, Ethiopian Flavours, where chefs cook up Ethiopian curries, vegetables and rice. The owner, Davide Ghetaceu, gave us his recipe for home-cooked doro alicha tibs, an Ethiopian chicken curry. Simple to make, it is incredibly tasty.

Heat the oil in a large saucepan over a medium heat, then add the onion and sauté for 8–10 minutes, until golden. Reduce the heat, add the ginger, garlic, paprika, cardamom, and cinnamon, and cook until well combined, about 2 minutes.

Add the chicken along with a good pinch of salt, and stir until well coated in the spices. Increase the heat to medium-high, and cook for about 10 minutes, stirring, until the chicken is browned and well-sealed all over.

Add the tomato, reduce the heat to low, and cook, stirring often, for about 10 minutes or until the chicken is cooked through. Towards the end of cooking, if the pan is very dry, add a splash of water, but bear in mind this is a relatively dry curry.

Sprinkle with the sliced green chili peppers, and serve with rice, a salad, cooked green beans, or cabbage.

≡ TIP ≡

If you don't have ground cardamom, pop the seeds out of 4 green cardamom pods and grind to a powder in a mortar and pestle.

CURRIED SHRIMP STIR-FRY

SERVES 4 WITH OTHER DISHES
PREP TIME: 20 MINS • COOK TIME: 20 MINS
WF • GF • DF • NF • SoF

FOR THE CURRY POWDER:

seeds from 4 **green cardamom pods**

2 **cloves**

¼ teaspoon **fennel seeds**

¼ teaspoon **cumin seeds**

¼ teaspoon **coriander seeds**

¼ teaspoon **ground turmeric**

¼ teaspoon **ground cinnamon**

¼ teaspoon **crushed red pepper**

FOR THE CURRY:

1 tablespoon **neutral cooking oil**

1 **onion**, finely sliced

1 clove of **garlic**, crushed

1 teaspoon peeled and finely grated
ginger

6 **curry leaves**

1 **green chili pepper** (deseeded or not, to taste), finely chopped

1 teaspoon **tomato paste**

1 pound **large shrimp** (fresh, or frozen and defrosted), peeled

a drop of **tamarind paste** or **concentrate**

salt, to taste

Loosely inspired by shrimp curries found in Malaysia and Indonesia, this stir-fried dry curry can also be turned into a soupy coconut curry— just add 7 ounces of coconut milk after the curry powder and bring up to a simmer, then add some salt, as needed.

Place all the curry powder ingredients in a mortar and pestle or spice grinder and pummel to a fine powder. Set aside.

Heat the oil in a wide skillet over a medium heat. Add the onion, and sauté for about 8 minutes, until the onion begins to brown. Add a pinch of salt, the garlic, ginger, curry leaves, green chili pepper, and tomato paste, and cook for 5 minutes, stirring constantly. Add the curry powder and cook for 1 minute, then add the shrimp and tamarind and sauté for 5 minutes, or until the shrimp are pink, cooked through, and well coated in the spice mixture.

Remove from the heat and serve immediately.

═ TIP ═

For a vegan version, omit the shrimp and cook 2–3 diced eggplants along with the onion, adding a splash of water towards the end of cooking if the pan seems very dry.

= TIP =

Don't use jackfruit in syrup by mistake—the can (or, occasionally, packet) must say "young" or "unripe green jackfruit in brine" or "water."

SRI LANKAN-STYLE JACKFRUIT CURRY

SERVES 4
PREP TIME: 20 MINS • COOK TIME: 45 MINS
WF • GF • DF • V • Ve • NF • SoF

1 tablespoon **neutral cooking oil**, plus a splash

2 **onions**, 1 finely sliced and 1 finely diced

1½ teaspoons **mustard seeds**

10 **curry leaves**, divided

a generous pinch of **crushed red pepper**

a generous pinch of **cumin seeds**

14 ounces **canned unripe green jackfruit**, drained and rinsed

1-inch piece of **ginger**, peeled and grated

2 cloves of **garlic**, crushed

1 **green chili pepper**, finely chopped

½ teaspoon **ground turmeric**

¼ teaspoon **cayenne pepper**

10 ounces **cauliflower**, broken into florets

1¾ cups **coconut milk**

½ teaspoon **tamarind paste**

a pinch of **sugar**

5 ounces **Chinese long beans**, trimmed

5 ounces **okra**, trimmed and sliced into ½-inch pieces (optional)

½–1 teaspoon **Sri Lankan roasted curry powder** (see page 106) or **hot Madras curry powder**

salt and **freshly ground black pepper**

rice or **Indian flatbreads** (pages 198–201 and 205–206), to serve

We only discovered jackfruit when we wrote our **Fast Vegan** *cookbook, because the unripe green fruit (sold ready-cooked in cans or packets) is an amazing meat substitute. We do feel a* **tiny** *bit silly: Southeast Asian, especially Sri Lankan, cooks have been using it for centuries.*

Heat 1 tablespoon oil in a large heavy skillet with a lid over a medium heat. Add the sliced onion and sauté for 10 minutes, until starting to brown. Add 1 teaspoon of the mustard seeds, the curry leaves, crushed red pepper, and cumin seeds, and cook for a further 5 minutes. The onions should be well browned and the mustard seeds should start to crackle. Remove from the heat, scrape into a bowl, and set aside.

Meanwhile, prepare the jackfruit. Discard the woody core and any large seeds, and shred the softer flesh. Set aside.

Add a splash more oil to the pan with the chopped onion and cook for 8 minutes, until translucent, then add the ginger, garlic, green chili pepper, and remaining mustard seeds. Cook for 5 minutes, stirring (the mustard seeds should pop as before), then add the turmeric and cayenne. Cook for 1 minute, reduce the heat, and add the cauliflower, jackfruit, coconut milk, tamarind paste, sugar, and some salt and pepper. Slowly bring to a simmer and cook for 10 minutes.

Add the beans and okra, if using, along with ½ teaspoon of curry powder. Mix well, then cover and cook for 5 minutes, until the vegetables are crisp-tender, apart from the jackfruit, which should be melting into the sauce. Remove from the heat. Stir about one-third of the onion mixture through the curry, then taste and add a little more salt, pepper, cayenne, or roasted curry powder, as needed. Serve topped with the remaining onions, with rice or Indian flatbreads.

THAI-STYLE CLAM CURRY

SERVES 4

PREP TIME: 15 MINS • COOK TIME: 17 MINS

WF • GF • DF • NF • SoF

1 tablespoon **neutral cooking oil**

1 **onion**, finely sliced

a pinch of **salt**

1 **lemongrass stalk**, outer layer and hard stem removed, finely chopped

2 cloves of **garlic**, crushed

2 **red chili peppers**, finely chopped

2 heaped teaspoons **nam prik pao** (Thai roasted chili paste)

14 ounces **coconut milk** (from a well-shaken can)

2 teaspoons **fish sauce**, or more to taste

6 **lime leaves**, torn

½ teaspoon **tamarind paste** or **concentrate**

2¼ pounds **fresh live clams**

a handful of **Thai basil leaves** (optional)

lime wedges, to serve (optional)

steamed rice or **Thai noodles**, to serve

═ TIP ═

If you want to add vegetables, use sliced baby corn, canned bamboo shoots, fine ribbons of carrot, shredded greens, or finely sliced bell peppers. They can all be added at the same time as the lemongrass and garlic.

Nam prik pao, a Thai roasted chili paste, is a powerhouse of an ingredient and is now widely available. Use it on its own to add a wallop of flavor to stir-fries, or mix with coconut milk in curries.

Heat the oil in a large heavy saucepan with a lid, set over a medium heat. Add the onion and salt and cook for about 8 minutes, until softened. Add the lemongrass, garlic, and chili pepper, and cook for 1 minute, then add the nam prik pao and stir well. Add the coconut milk to the mixture with the fish sauce, lime leaves, and tamarind (be careful not to add too much tamarind as it will overwhelm everything, given the chance). Gently bring to a simmer, then taste—the broth should be spicy, savory, and tangy. Add more fish sauce, if needed, remembering that the clams will bring their own salty-sweetness in a moment.

Increase the heat and bring the curry to a simmer. Tip the clams into the pan and cover with the lid. Cook for 3½ minutes, giving the pan a firm jiggle once or twice. Remove the lid and discard any clams that have remained closed. Stir through half of the Thai basil leaves, if using.

Serve the clams and their wonderful curry broth in shallow bowls, with rice or noodles on the side. Top with the rest of the Thai basil leaves and give each diner a wedge of lime to squeeze over, and a spoon.

EGGPLANT AND TOMATO CURRY

SERVES 2 AS A MAIN OR 4 AS A SIDE

PREP TIME: 15 MINS • COOK TIME: 30 MINS

WF • GF • DF • V • Ve • NF • SoF • SUITABLE FOR FREEZING

2 medium **eggplants**

1 tablespoon **neutral cooking oil**

2 cloves of **garlic**, crushed

1-inch piece of **ginger**, peeled and finely grated

1 **green chili pepper** (deseeded or not, to taste), finely chopped

1 teaspoon **ground cumin**

1 teaspoon **ground coriander**

1 teaspoon **ground turmeric**

¼–½ teaspoon **chili powder**, to taste

1 teaspoon **fennel seeds**

14 ounces **canned diced tomatoes**, undrained

¾ cup **water**

a generous pinch of **sugar**

salt and **freshly ground black pepper**

a handful of **fresh cilantro**

Very, very easy and very, very tasty.

Trim the eggplants, then cut in half crossways through the middle. Cut into finger-sized wedges and trim any seedy parts of the flesh (otherwise they will expand during cooking and you will end up with threads of seeds trailing through the finished curry).

Heat the oil in a large saucepan with a lid, set over a medium heat. When hot, add the garlic, ginger, and chili pepper, and cook, stirring, for 3 minutes. Stir in the cumin, coriander, turmeric, chili powder, and fennel seeds, and gently cook for 2 minutes, then add the tomatoes, water, eggplant wedges, sugar, and a pinch of salt and some freshly ground black pepper. Push the eggplant wedges into the liquid, then cover with the lid, bring up to a merry simmer, and cook for about 15 minutes.

Remove the lid—the eggplant wedges will have collapsed into the curry. Increase the heat a little and let the sauce reduce for about 10 minutes.

Remove from the heat and check that the eggplant wedges are meltingly tender, then stir through the cilantro leaves before serving.

═ TIP ═

Bulk this out by adding cooked chickpeas, cubes of paneer or firm tofu, or roasted sweet peppers from a jar (in oil).

SLOW

LAMB ROGAN JOSH

SERVES 4

PREP TIME: 10 MINS, PLUS 20 MINS–8 HOURS MARINATING • COOK TIME: 50 MINS

WF • GF • DF (if substituting the yogurt) **• NF** (if using dairy yogurt) **• SoF • SUITABLE FOR FREEZING**

1¾ pounds boneless **lamb shoulder**, cut into bite-size chunks, fat trimmed

5 heaped tablespoons **whole-milk plain yogurt** (or a nondairy yogurt)

1½-inch piece of **ginger**, peeled and finely grated

½ teaspoon **chili powder**

2 teaspoons **paprika**

a generous pinch of **salt**

1 tablespoon **neutral cooking oil**

¼ teaspoon **ground mace**

½ teaspoon **asafetida**

5 **cloves**

seeds from 4 **green cardamom pods**

½ teaspoon **fennel seeds**

a generous grinding of **black pepper**

a pinch of **saffron**

1 cup **hot water**

rice, to serve (optional)

a small handful of **fresh cilantro**, to garnish (optional)

≡ TIP ≡

If you can get your hands on brick-red Kashmiri chili powder, which is pretty mild, use it instead of our paprika-and-chili mix.

We wanted this recipe to be close to the Kashmiri original, which doesn't contain onions, garlic or tomatoes. You do need the asafetida powder to give it an onion-y flavor; if you don't have any, soften a finely chopped onion in the oil for 10 minutes before adding the lamb. (This recipe is loosely based on one by the brilliant food writer Maunika Gowardhan.)

Place the lamb in a bowl with the yogurt, ginger, chili powder, and paprika and a generous pinch of salt. Mix to coat the lamb, then marinate in the fridge for at least 20 minutes, although overnight is even better.

Heat the oil in a large deep saucepan with a lid, set over a medium heat. When hot, add the lamb and its marinade, and cook until the lamb is lightly browned all over and the marinade has reduced, about 8–10 minutes.

Meanwhile, place all the spices in a mortar and pestle or a spice grinder and grind until smooth and well combined.

Reduce the heat to low and add the spices to the pan. Cook, stirring often, for about 10 minutes, until really fragrant.

Meanwhile, soak the saffron in the hot water for about 5 minutes, then pour the mixture into the pan. Bring to a gentle simmer, then cover and gently cook for about 20 minutes.

Finally, remove the lid and let the sauce (which should be quite thin even at the end of cooking) reduce by about half; about a further 10 minutes.

Serve with rice and sprinkled with the fresh cilantro leaves, if desired.

TIP

A version of this is made with waxy potatoes cooked in the curry, which is irresistible.

BEEF RENDANG

SERVES 4

PREP TIME: 25 MINS • COOK TIME: 3 HOURS

WF • GF • DF • NF • SoF • SUITABLE FOR FREEZING

1 tablespoon **neutral cooking oil**

1½ tablespoons **tamarind paste**

2 **cloves**

3 **green cardamom pods**

¾-inch stick of **cinnamon**

1 teaspoon **sugar**

1¾ pounds **beef shank**, cut into chunks

1¾ cups **coconut milk**

½ cup **water**

1 stalk **lemongrass**, bruised

5 **lime leaves**, roughly torn

4½ tablespoons **desiccated coconut**

crushed red pepper, to taste

salt, to taste

FOR THE CURRY PASTE:

1 large **onion**, finely chopped

4 cloves of **garlic**, crushed

1 **lemongrass stalk**, outer layer removed,
    finely chopped

1½-inch piece of **ginger**, peeled and grated

1 teaspoon **galangal paste**, or peeled and
    very finely chopped fresh galangal

2–3 small **dried red chili peppers**,
    crumbled

1 **fresh red chili pepper**, deseeded and
    finely chopped

a generous pinch of **salt**

This incredible slow-cooked beef curry is associated with both Indonesia and Malaysia—in fact, John was taught how to make it by a fantastic cook called Chef Ann in Malaysia, while on holiday with Katie and their kids (Chef Ann's recipes also appear in our Family & Friends *cookbook). The scent of it cooking is almost as good as the eating.*

Use a small blender or mortar and pestle to grind the curry paste ingredients until fairly smooth. Add 1 tablespoon of water if needed to loosen the mixture.

Heat the oil in a large heavy saucepan with a lid, set over a low-medium heat. When hot, add the curry paste and fry for 3 minutes, stirring constantly, until fragrant and sizzling. Add the tamarind concentrate, cloves, cardamom pods, cinnamon stick, and sugar, and continue to fry for another 5 minutes.

Add the beef, coconut milk, water, lemongrass, lime leaves, and a generous pinch of salt, gently bring to a simmer (so that the coconut milk doesn't separate), then cover and cook for 2½–3 hours, until the beef is meltingly tender and the sauce has reduced to a dark brown, thick gravy.

About 10 minutes before serving, place a dry skillet over a medium heat. When hot, add the desiccated coconut and toast, stirring constantly, until golden, being sure to toss the coconut enough that the bottom flakes don't burn. Stir the coconut into the curry.

Taste and add more salt or crushed red pepper, as needed. Serve with plain steamed or coconut rice (see page 168), with some garlicky sautéed greens on the side.

SLOW

LAMB DHANSAK

SERVES 4

PREP TIME: 25 MINS • COOK TIME: 2 HOURS

WF • GF • DF • NF • SoF • SUITABLE FOR FREEZING

3 ounces **white split urid/urad dal lentils**
(optional)

2 ounces (or 5 ounces) **yellow split peas**

2 ounces **red split lentils**

½ teaspoon **coriander seeds**

¼ teaspoon **cumin seeds**

seeds from 3 **green cardamom pods**

3 **cloves**

½ teaspoon **fennel seeds**

a pinch of **fenugreek seeds**

¼ teaspoon **ground cinnamon**

½ teaspoon **ground turmeric**

a pinch of **freshly grated nutmeg**

a pinch of **freshly ground black pepper**

1 tablespoon **neutral cooking oil**

2 **onions**, finely chopped

4 cloves of **garlic**, crushed or finely grated

1½-inch piece of **ginger**, peeled and finely
grated

1 pound **lamb shoulder**, diced

4 ounces **fresh tomatoes**, chopped

1 tablespoon each **finely chopped green
chili pepper**, **fresh dill**, **fresh mint**, and
fresh cilantro

1 tablespoon **tamarind paste**

2 ounces **frozen fenugreek leaves**
(optional)

up to ½ teaspoon **salt**, or to taste

*Traditionally, this Parsi lamb and lentil stew is made with toor dal
(pigeon peas), but split peas work just as well.*

Wash the lentils and pick over for debris. Place in a large lidded saucepan with 4¼
cups of hot water and bring to a fast boil. Boil for 5 minutes, skimming off any scum,
then reduce the heat, cover, and simmer for 25 minutes.

Use a mortar and pestle or spice grinder to grind the whole spices, then mix together
with the ground spices. Set aside. Heat the oven to 275°F.

Heat the oil in a large, deep, ovenproof saucepan with a lid over a medium heat. Add
the onions, and cook for 10 minutes, stirring often, until slightly browned. Add the
garlic, ginger, and spice mixture, and cook for 2 minutes, stirring. Add the lamb and
cook, stirring, for 5 minutes, until slightly browned. Add the tomatoes and cook for
5 minutes, stirring now and then. Add the chili pepper, herbs (saving a little of each
herb to garnish), tamarind, and fenugreek leaves, if using.

Ladle the lentils into the onion pan. If it seems dry, add a little water. Bring to a
simmer, then cover and cook in the oven for 1 hour. Check the lamb at this point and
return to the oven for 15–30 minutes as necessary—you want it to be falling apart.

To thicken the sauce, scoop 4 ladles of the lentils, vegetables, and broth (leaving the
meat in the pan) into a food processor and blitz until smooth, then return to the pan.
If it still seems a little thin, place on the heat and simmer to reduce.

Add ¼ teaspoon of salt, then taste to see if you want more (or more chili pepper for
heat, or tamarind for sourness). Serve, sprinkled with the remaining herbs, with rice
or Indian flatbreads (see pages 198–201 and 205–206).

= TIP =

If you prefer, you can make this in one pot, but lentil cooking times can be unpredictable when mixed with other things, so we like to get them started on their own. Try adding diced eggplant or squash along with the onion, or add a handful of finely chopped spinach 5 minutes before serving.

≡ TIP ≡

Urid/urad dal is easy to find in Asian supermarkets and online—just make sure you choose the black variety for this dish, rather than the white.

BLACK DHAL MAKHANI

SERVES 4
PREP TIME: 15 MINS, PLUS 8 HOURS SOAKING • COOK TIME: 6 HOURS
WF • GF • V • NF • SoF (check flatbreads) • **SUITABLE FOR FREEZING**

7 ounces **dried black lentils** (urid/urad dal), soaked for 8 hours or overnight in cold water, drained, and rinsed

3 teaspoons of **butter** or **ghee**

5 **cloves**

4 **green cardamom pods**

¼ teaspoon **fennel seeds**

½ teaspoon **cumin seeds**

1 teaspoon **garam masala**

¼ teaspoon **ground cinnamon**

¼ teaspoon **chili powder**

1-inch piece of **ginger**, peeled and finely grated

2 cloves of **garlic**, crushed

½ **green chili pepper**, deseeded and finely chopped

1 **onion**, finely chopped

1 tablespoon **tomato paste**

1 **bay leaf**

1 teaspoon **brown sugar**

4 ounces **canned kidney beans**, drained and rinsed

4 tablespoons **heavy cream**

salt, to taste

a handful of **fresh cilantro**, to garnish

pappadams or **Indian flatbreads** (see pages 198–201 and 205–206), to serve

Don't be put off by the length of time this Punjabi dhal takes to make— you barely need to look at it once it's cooking and it really, truly, is worth the wait. We wrote this recipe for **LEON Happy Soups** *a few years ago—our own version of the famous Dishoom classic.*

Place the lentils and 3 cups hot water in a nonreactive saucepan with a lid, bring to a fast boil, and cook for 5 minutes. Skim off any scum, reduce the heat, cover, and cook for 30–40 minutes, until the lentils are soft and beginning to break down.

Melt 1 teaspoon of the butter or ghee in a large ovenproof saucepan with a lid, set over a low heat. Add the cardamom pods, fennel, cumin, garam masala, cinnamon, and chili powder. Cook, stirring, for 2 minutes, then add the ginger and garlic, and cook for 1–2 minutes. Add 1 more teaspoon of butter, the green chili pepper, onion, a pinch of salt, and the tomato paste and cook for about 10 minutes, stirring often, until the onion is soft. Remove from the heat, add the bay leaf and sugar, and set aside.

Heat the oven to 275°F.

Roughly mash the kidney beans and add to the onion pan. Ladle the lentils and their cooking liquid into the same pan, then cover and cook in the oven for 4–5 hours, or longer if you can, adding 3–4 tablespoons of water every hour, and stirring the contents of the pan to prevent sticking.

When ready, the dhal will be very creamy, and the longer you leave it, the deeper brown it will be. Remove from the oven and stir in the cream and the remaining butter, plus enough hot water to loosen it to a thick soup. Taste and add a little more salt, if necessary. Remove the bay leaf and cardamom pods. Garnish with fresh cilantro and eat with papadums or wedges of Indian flatbreads for dunking.

BUTTERNUT, CHICKPEA, & KALE CURRY

SERVES 4

PREP TIME: 25 MINS • COOK TIME: 55 MINS

WF • GF • DF • V • Ve • NF • SoF

2 tablespoons **neutral cooking oil**

1 teaspoon **mustard seeds**

2 teaspoons **cumin seeds**

1 teaspoon **crushed red pepper**

1 teaspoon **coriander seeds**

6 **cloves**

6 **green cardamom pods**

2 **onions**, finely diced

3 cloves of **garlic**, crushed

1½-inch piece of **ginger**, peeled and finely grated

2 tablespoons **tomato paste**

1 pound **butternut squash**, peeled, deseeded, and cut into ¾-inch chunks

14 ounces **canned chickpeas**, drained

14 ounces **hot water** (or enough to cover)

9 ounces **kale** or **cavolo nero**, stems removed, leaves finely shredded

freshly squeezed lemon juice, to taste

salt and **freshly ground black pepper**

a handful of **fresh cilantro**, to garnish

rice, to serve

We first made this with lamb, but found we love this vegan version more. We also love serving it with Black Rice (see page 169).

Heat the oil in a large deep saucepan with a lid, set over a medium heat. Add the mustard seeds and, when they start to pop, reduce the heat and add the cumin, crushed red pepper, coriander seeds, cloves, cardamom pods, and onions. Cook for about 8 minutes, stirring, until the spices are very fragrant and the onions are soft. Add the garlic, ginger, and tomato paste and cook for about 3 minutes, stirring, until the raw smell is cooked out. Add a pinch of salt, the butternut squash, chickpeas, and enough hot water to cover. Cover with the lid and gently simmer for 25–35 minutes, until the squash is tender. Remove the lid and stir well, letting the squash break down a little to thicken the sauce.

Add the kale or cavolo nero to the pan, pushing it down to submerge it in the sauce. Increase the heat and simmer for 5 minutes.

Squeeze over a little lemon juice, then taste for salt and pepper. Serve with rice, sprinkled with a handful of fresh cilantro leaves.

== TIP ==

In season, pumpkins and gourds are delicious in this—look for more exciting varieties and colors than the ubiquitous butternut squash.

KUKU PAKA WITH UGALI

SERVES 4

PREP TIME: 25 MINS • COOK TIME: 1 HOUR 5 MINS

WF • GF • DF • NF • SoF

2 tablespoons **neutral cooking oil**

4 skin-on **whole chicken legs**, or 8 bone-in, skin-on **thighs** and **drumsticks**

2 **onions**, finely chopped

4 cloves of **garlic**, crushed

1-inch piece of **ginger**, peeled and finely grated

3 **green chili peppers** (deseeded or not, to taste), finely chopped

1 tablespoon **tomato paste**

2 teaspoons **ground cumin**

2 teaspoons **ground coriander**

1½ teaspoons **ground turmeric**

2 x 13½-ounce cans **coconut milk** (cans well-shaken)

1 teaspoon **tamarind paste** or **concentrate** (or add **freshly squeezed lemon juice** at the end of cooking)

salt and **freshly ground black pepper**

a handful of **fresh cilantro**, to garnish

This is a Kenyan-style chicken curry, where roasting the meat beforehand results in deliciously crispy skin. When Rebecca first tried it, working in Kenya in 2007, she ate it with ugali—a thick, creamy cornmeal. (She also went skinny-dipping for the first and only time, but that's another story!)

Heat the oven to 375°F.

Pour 1 tablespoon of the oil into a roasting pan (in which all the chicken can fit in a single snug layer), then add the chicken. Roast for 40 minutes, basting once with the juices, halfway through.

Meanwhile, make the sauce. Add the other tablespoon of oil to a saucepan set over a medium heat. When hot, add the onions and cook for about 8 minutes, until softened and just starting to brown. Add the garlic, ginger, and green chili peppers, and cook for 2–3 minutes, until fragrant, then add the tomato paste. Cook, stirring, for 2 minutes, then add the ground spices and cook for 1 minute, just to toast them briefly. Pour in the coconut milk and add the tamarind, if using. Stir well and remove from the heat. If the chicken still has longer to cook, set the sauce aside.

To make the ugali, pour the water into a large high-sided saucepan and bring back to a boil. Pour in the cornmeal/polenta in a steady stream, stirring quickly, to prevent lumps forming. Cook, stirring all the time, until smooth and very thick. Taste—it will be very bland and shouldn't be gritty. Continue to cook, still stirring often, until the mixture is thick enough to pull away from the sides of the pan, about 15 minutes. Set aside, off the heat, to firm up for a few minutes while the chicken finishes cooking.

FOR THE UGALI:

3¼–3¾ cups **freshly boiled water**

9 ounces **coarse white** (or **yellow**) **cornmeal/polenta** (not "quick-cooking")

FOR THE GREENS:

14 ounces **kale**, **spring greens**, **large leaf spinach,** or **chard**, tough stems removed, finely shredded and freshly washed

1 **red chili pepper**, finely diced

salt and **freshly ground black pepper**

Don't cook the ugali too far in advance, as it will set. (Traditionally, no salt or pepper is added to ugali, but feel free to, if you prefer.)

Remove the roasted chicken from the oven. Spoon off any excess fat, if there is a lot in the pan, but leave the cooking juices behind. Pour the curry sauce over the chicken, spooning some sauce over each piece. Arrange so that the chicken pieces are all sitting skin-side up with the skin out of the sauce, and return to the oven for a final 10 minutes to crisp up.

Meanwhile, set a large skillet over a high heat and add a splash of oil. When hot, add the wet greens and the chili pepper. Sauté until wilted, then remove from the heat and drain (if necessary). Keep warm until ready to serve.

Use two large serving spoons to shape the ugali into firm, neat oblongs, about the size and shape of a small baked potato. Serve these and the greens alongside the chicken, with the curry sauce spooned over the meat. Finish with a squeeze of lemon, if you didn't use tamarind, and garnish with a handful of cilantro leaves.

≡ TIP ≡

For more richly flavored greens, sauté 1 diced onion, 1 crushed clove of garlic, and 1 teaspoon of tomato paste in the pan first, then braise the wet greens, covered with a lid, for 5 minutes or so.

CHICKEN DOPIAZA

SERVES 4
PREP TIME: 15 MINS • COOK TIME: 1¼ HOURS
WF • GF • DF (if substituting the yogurt) **• NF • SoF** (check flatbreads) **• SUITABLE FOR FREEZING**

2 tablespoons **neutral cooking oil**

3 **onions**, 2 finely sliced, 1 cut into
¾-inch chunks

7 tablespoons **whole-milk plain yogurt**
(substitute nondairy yogurt,
if wished)

¼ teaspoon **chili powder**

1 teaspoon **sweet paprika**

1 teaspoon **ground turmeric**

1¾ pounds bone-in **chicken thighs** and
drumsticks (skin on or off)

1-inch piece of **ginger**, peeled and grated

2 cloves of **garlic**, crushed

½ teaspoon **ground coriander**

¼ teaspoon **ground cinnamon**

½ teaspoon **ground cumin**

6 **green cardamom pods**

14 ounces **canned diced tomatoes**

2 medium **green chili peppers**, slit
lengthways

freshly squeezed lemon juice

salt and **freshly ground black pepper**

warm flatbreads or **steamed basmati
rice**, to serve

*This is an Afghani dish. The name means "two onions"—the first lot are
browned and the second simmered and softened in the tangy sauce.*

Heat the oil in a large saucepan with a lid, set over a medium heat. Add the sliced
onions and cook for 15–20 minutes, stirring often, until dark golden and sticky-
looking—turn the heat to low if they start to burn.

Meanwhile, stir together 6 tablespoons of the yogurt with the chili powder, paprika,
and turmeric, then add the chicken and marinate briefly while the onions cook.

Add the ginger, garlic, coriander, cinnamon, cumin, and cardamom pods to the pan
and cook for 1–2 minutes, stirring all the time, until fragrant. Tip the chicken and
marinade into the pan, and cook for about 5 minutes, still stirring, until the onions
and yogurt have cooked together to form a thick, fragrant, oily-looking paste.

Add the tomatoes and cook for 3–4 minutes, using the tomato juice to deglaze the
pan and scrape up anything that has stuck to the bottom. Pour in 1¼ cups hot water
and add the chili peppers, plus a little salt and pepper. Bring to a simmer, then reduce
the heat, cover with the lid, and cook for 30 minutes.

Remove the lid and add the onion chunks. Increase the heat to allow the extra liquid
to reduce and cook for 15 minutes.

Check that the chicken is cooked through and the onion chunks are beautifully
soft. Remove the pan from the heat and let stand for 5 minutes. Just before serving,
stir through the last tablespoon of yogurt and a little squeeze of lemon juice. Serve
with flatbreads or rice.

≡ TIP ≡

As with many curries, you could make this with other meats or fish. If using lamb, just increase the simmering time and make sure there is enough liquid for the extra time. If using fish, don't marinate it in the yogurt, and add to the curry 5 minutes before the end of cooking.

≡ **TIP** ≡

This freezes well and leftovers can be used to fill pitas or wraps, or even stirred into spiced scrambled eggs or omelets.

MATT'S LAMB KEEMA WITH WHOLE SPICES, METHI, & PEAS

SERVES 4
PREP TIME: 15 MINS • COOK TIME: 55 MINS
WF • GF • NF • SoF

1-inch stick of **cinnamon**

3 **green cardamon pods**

7 **black peppercorns**

3 **cloves**

½ teaspoon **cumin seeds**

4 tablespoons **rapeseed oil**, or any
   neutral cooking oil

2 **red onions**, diced

3 cloves of **garlic**, crushed to a paste

1-inch piece of **ginger**, peeled and finely
   grated

1 pound **ground lamb**

2 teaspoons **ground coriander**

1 teaspoon **ground cumin**

1–1½ teaspoons **chili powder**

½ teaspoon **ground turmeric**

1 tablespoon **dried fenugreek leaves**
   (methi)

3 tablespoons **whole-milk plain yogurt**

5 tablespoons **tomato purée**

1½ teaspoons **salt**

9 ounces **frozen peas**

steamed **basmati rice** and **Dhal** (see
   pages 26 or 79), to serve

Matt Sefton and his partner Carmel were "best people" to Steve (who photographed the food in this book), when he married Rebecca (who helped write this book). Years before that, Matt taught Steve how to cook when they lived in a house-share in Brixton—for which Rebecca is forever grateful. This is Matt's recipe for lamb keema, which he likes to serve with a smoky, garlicky dhal and basmati rice.

Dry-fry the whole spices in a wide skillet with a lid, set over a high heat. After about 30 seconds, add the oil and the onions and cook for 7–8 minutes, until the onions are turning golden at the edges. Add the garlic and ginger and cook for 1–2 minutes, until fragrant. Push the onion mixture to the side of the pan and add the lamb, breaking it up with a spoon as you go. Cook for about 10 minutes, stirring often, until no traces of pink remain and most of the liquid has evaporated.

Add the ground spices and the fenugreek leaves, and cook for a few moments, then reduce the heat to medium and slowly stir in the yogurt, then add the purée and the salt.

Reduce the heat to low, cover with the lid, and cook for about 25–30 minutes, stirring frequently. Just before the end of cooking, add the frozen peas and cook through. Serve with basmati rice and dhal.

CHICKEN BIRYANI

SERVES 4

PREP TIME: 25 MINS, PLUS 40 MINS–24 HOURS MARINATING • COOK TIME: 1 HOUR 10 MINS

WF • GF • NF • SoF

1½ pounds skinless, boneless **chicken thighs**, cut into large chunks

FOR THE CHICKEN MARINADE:

4 heaped tablespoons **whole-milk Greek yogurt**

1-inch piece of **ginger**, peeled and finely grated

2 cloves of **garlic**, peeled and finely grated or crushed

½ teaspoon **salt**

½ teaspoon **paprika**

½ teaspoon **chili powder**

1 tablespoon **finely chopped mint leaves**

1 tablespoon **finely chopped fresh cilantro**

½ teaspoon **ground coriander**

½ teaspoon **ground cumin**

FOR THE BIRYANI:

7 ounces **basmati rice**

2 cups **water**

4 **green cardamom pods**

2 **cloves**

2 tablespoons **neutral cooking oil**

2 **onions**, finely sliced

½ cup **milk**

This dish is a real show-stopper. It looks much more complex to prepare than it really is—you just need to get each part ready before layering it together and throwing it in the oven for half an hour.

Mix all the chicken marinade ingredients together, then stir in the chicken. Cover and place in the fridge to marinate for as long as you can—40 minutes–24 hours.

About 40 minutes before you want to cook, prepare the rice. Rinse the rice several times in running water, then cover with cold water and leave to soak for 20 minutes. Drain.

Set a large saucepan over a high heat and add the measured water, cardamom pods, cloves, and a generous pinch of salt. Bring to a boil, then add the drained rice to the pan. Cook for 7 minutes, until about half-done, then remove from the heat, drain again, and set aside. Remove and discard the whole spices.

Meanwhile, set a large heavy ovenproof saucepan with a very well-fitting lid over a medium heat. Add 1 tablespoon of the oil and the onions and cook for 20–30 minutes, stirring often, until the onions are caramelized, deep brown, sticky, and soft. Remove from the pan and set aside.

While the rice and onions are cooking, make the masala spice mix, if using. Set a small saucepan over a medium heat and add the bay leaf, cloves, fennel, cumin, coriander, and cardamom seeds. Toast just until the whole spices are fragrant, taking care not

RECIPE CONTINUES →

a generous pinch of **saffron**

salt, to taste

a handful each of **fresh cilantro** and **mint**, roughly torn, plus extra to serve

freshly squeezed lemon juice, to serve

FOR THE BIRYANI MASALA (IF USING—SEE TIP):

1 **bay leaf**

3 **cloves**

¼ teaspoon **fennel seeds**

¼ teaspoon **cumin seeds**

¼ teaspoon **coriander seeds**

seeds from 6 **green cardamom pods**

¼ teaspoon **crushed red pepper**

¼ teaspoon **ground mace**

¼ teaspoon **ground cinnamon**

generous dusting of **freshly grated nutmeg**

generous grinding of **black pepper**

to burn them. Immediately tip it all into a mortar and pestle or spice grinder and add the crushed red pepper, mace, cinnamon, nutmeg, and black pepper. Grind to a powder—you may need to remove and discard the tough stem of the bay leaf. Set aside.

Place the ovenproof pan that you used to cook the onions back on a medium heat, and add the remaining 1 tablespoon of oil. Add the chicken and its marinade, plus 2 heaped teaspoons of the biryani masala, and cook for 7–8 minutes, stirring and turning each piece of meat once or twice.

Warm the milk and add the saffron, to infuse.

Heat the oven to 350°F.

Assemble the biryani by arranging the chicken in a single, even layer in the bottom of its pan. Cover with half of the rice, evenly spread out. Drizzle over half of the infused saffron milk. Sprinkle over half of the cilantro and mint and half of the caramelized onions. Repeat. Sprinkle over a pinch of salt, then place a layer of parchment paper over the pan and set the lid on top, to form a tight seal. Place in the oven and cook for 30 minutes.

Ideally, take straight to the table and remove the lid there, as it will release a cloud of amazingly fragrant steam. Squeeze over a little lemon juice and garnish with a little extra cilantro and mint, just before serving. Eat immediately.

≡ TIP ≡

You can use ready-made biryani masala spice mix—making it fresh gives the richest flavor, but it's easy to track down in supermarkets.

EMILY'S AMAZING BIRMINGHAM BALTI

SERVES 4–6

PREP TIME: 20 MINS • COOK TIME: 2–8 HOURS

NF • SoF (check naan)

3 tablespoons **neutral cooking oil**, plus
extra for greasing

1 **whole chicken**, or 6–8 bone-in **thighs**
(skin on or off)

3–4 **onions** (more if you want a less saucy
curry), cut into chunks

3 cloves of **garlic**, crushed (or more,
to taste)

1½-inch piece of **ginger**, peeled and diced

1 large **tomato**, finely diced

2 teaspoons **garam masala**

1 teaspoon **ground coriander**

½ teaspoon **chili powder** (or more,
to taste)

a generous pinch of **salt**

1 teaspoon **ground turmeric**

¾ cup **water**, or more as needed

Naan (see page 198), to serve

a handful of **fresh cilantro**, to garnish

*Birmingham is famous for baltis—there's no taste like it. A native
"Brummie," Emily Hawkley is LEON's operations manager: "I LIVE for
a good balti. The longer you can cook it the better. The reason Brummies
go for a curry at 2–3 a.m. is because it tastes AMAZING late-night, after
a few beers. It's cooked in huge pots all evening, then flashed over a hot
flame with your order just before serving."*

Heat the oven to 375°F. Lightly grease a roasting pan with oil.

Roast the chicken in the oiled pan, basting once or twice, until cooked through
(40–50 minutes for thighs; 1–1½ hours for a whole chicken, depending on size).
Remove from the oven and let cool. Strip all the meat from the bones and refrigerate
until ready to eat.

Meanwhile, heat the oil in a heavy saucepan with a lid over a medium-low heat. Add
the onions, garlic, and ginger and fry for about 10 minutes, until the onions are soft
and translucent, but not browned. Add the remaining ingredients, except the water.
Stir and cook for 3–5 minutes, until everything comes together and begins to look
saucy and oily. Add the water, bring to a simmer, and cook for 20–25 minutes, stirring
every now and then.

RECIPE CONTINUES ➡

For a quick curry, you can blend the sauce at this point, but ideally cook it slowly, covered with a lid, for several hours, or even all day over a *very* low heat (or in a slow cooker on low for 6–8 hours). Stir often, and add a splash of water if it gets too dry.

When ready to serve, you can leave the sauce as it is, or blend a little, or a lot for a smoother balti sauce. When you're happy, add the torn cooked chicken to the curry.

If you have small metal balti dishes for serving, place them over a high heat and flash the curry in individual portions, to heat and thicken. If not, reheat in the pan and serve in well-warmed bowls, with breads on the side for dipping. Sprinkle with fresh cilantro and ENJOY.

≡ TIP ≡

1. Good garam masala is key. Try your local international food store—it's worth the extra pennies.
2. Ideally, eat from a steel dish that you can heat over a flame. If not, make sure your bowl is hot before serving.
3. You can add any protein you like to this instead of the chicken—chickpeas, Curry-Spiced Tofu (see page 102), or pre-cooked meat. Alternatively, cook chunks of fish or shrimp directly in the sauce.

SIDES

ONION BHAJIS

MAKES ABOUT 30 BHAJIS
PREP TIME: 20 MINS • COOK TIME: 20–25 MINS
WF • GF • DF • V • VE • NF • SoF • SUITABLE FOR FREEZING

9 ounces **chickpea flour/besan**

1 teaspoon **ground turmeric**

½ teaspoon **garam masala**

¼ teaspoon **asafetida** or **garlic powder**
(optional)

2 tablespoons **roughly chopped fresh
cilantro**

1 medium **green chili pepper**, deseeded
and finely diced

¾–1¼ cups **cold water**

1 tablespoon **vegetable oil**, plus extra
for cooking

1 tablespoon **freshly squeezed lime juice**
(about ½ lime)

2 **onions**, quartered, then very finely
sliced

salt and **freshly ground black pepper**

Chutneys (see pages 215–217), **Raita**
(see pages 163–164), and/or **Tamarind
Yogurt** (see page 165), to serve

*This recipe makes a LOT of bhajis (also known as onion pakora or
pakoda), but they reheat very well; either refrigerate or freeze, then defrost
and crisp up in the oven at 400°F for 3–4 minutes.*

Mix all the dry ingredients together with ½ teaspoon of salt and some black pepper.
Add the cilantro and green chili pepper, then whisk in enough water to make a
smooth, thick batter. Add the oil and lime juice, then whisk again.

Mix the sliced onions and batter together.

Set a deep, high-sided skillet over a high heat and pour in a 2¼-inch depth of cooking
oil. Heat to 350°F (if you have a deep-fry thermometer), or until a cube of day-old
bread fizzes and browns in 30 seconds.

Carefully add a little bit of the mixture to the pan and cook for 1–2 minutes, until
golden. Cool slightly, then taste to check the seasoning.

Use a flat dessert spoon to scoop up 4 or 5 little parcels of the batter and onion and
slide gently into the hot oil. They should fizz merrily and then turn golden brown in
about 4 minutes—any quicker and the onion won't cook, so turn the heat down as
needed. Turn each bhaji in the oil at least once so they cook evenly.

Remove with a slotted spoon to drain further on a plate lined with paper towel. Keep
warm while you cook the rest. Serve with chutneys, raita, and/or tamarind yogurt.

═ TIP ═

Three words for you: onion
bhaji sandwiches. Just add
chutney and raita.

≡ TIP ≡

Don't skimp on the time this needs in
the food processor—beating the fish to
a paste gives the fishcakes that bouncy
texture you will know from
Thai restaurants.

THAI FISHCAKES

SERVES 4 AS A SIDE OR STARTER (MAKES 8–10 FISHCAKES)
PREP TIME: 20 MINS • COOK TIME: 15 MINS
WF • GF • DF • NF • SoF

9 ounces **white fish** (we like basa)

1 **egg white**

1½ tablespoons **Thai red curry paste** (see page 43, or store-bought)

a generous pinch of **sugar**

2 teaspoons **fish sauce**, or more to taste

2 ounces **Chinese long beans**, trimmed and finely chopped into ¼-inch pieces

3 **lime leaves**, stems removed, very finely chopped

neutral cooking oil, for frying

lime wedges, to serve

a handful of **fresh cilantro**, to garnish

FOR THE DIPPING SAUCE:

2 tablespoons **ready-made sweet chili sauce**

2 tablespoons **water**

4 teaspoons **fish sauce**

2 tablespoons finely chopped **cucumber**

1 tablespoon **very finely chopped roasted peanuts**

1 teaspoon **very finely chopped shallot**

We sort of wish we hadn't discovered how easy these are to make. Because now we can't stop.

Place the fish, egg white, curry paste, sugar, and fish sauce into a food processor and blitz for 4–5 minutes (depending on the power of your food processor), scraping down the sides a few times as needed, until completely smooth. You should have a pale pink purée with a fairly sticky texture. Stir in the beans and lime leaves and mix thoroughly.

Mix together the dipping sauce ingredients and set aside.

Pour a ½-inch depth of cooking oil into a skillet with fairly high sides. Heat until shimmering hot (about 350°F if you have a deep-fry thermometer).

Drop a nugget of the fishcake mixture into the hot oil and fry for about 1 minute, until golden and cooked through. Taste and decide whether the mixture needs more fish sauce. When happy with the flavor, shape the fishcakes into 2-inch round patties, using your hands (this is quite messy as the mix is sticky, so you can use two large spoons to shape, if you prefer).

Slide the patties into the hot oil and fry for about 2 minutes on each side, turning with a heat-resistant spatula, until a deep, golden brown. (Don't crowd the pan as the oil will cool down and the patties will cook too slowly and be greasy.) Remove from the oil with tongs, letting the excess oil drain back into the pan, and set to drain on a plate lined with paper towel while you cook the rest.

Serve with the dipping sauce and lime wedges, with cilantro leaves to garnish.

ALOO TIKKI

MAKES ABOUT 20

PREP TIME: 20 MINS, PLUS 1 HOUR CHILLING • COOK TIME: 35 MINS

WF • GF (if using gluten-free flour) • V • Ve (if using oil or vegan ghee) • NF • SoF • SUITABLE FOR FREEZING

all-purpose flour, for coating

salt and **freshly ground black pepper**

neutral cooking oil or **ghee**, for frying

FOR THE ALOO TIKKI MIXTURE:

2¼ pounds **floury potatoes**, unpeeled, cut into large chunks

1 tablespoon **neutral cooking oil**

1 teaspoon **black mustard seeds**

1 large **onion**, very finely diced

3 cloves of **garlic**, crushed

2-inch piece of **ginger**, peeled and finely grated

1 **green chili pepper** (deseeded or not, to taste), very finely chopped

½ teaspoon **ground turmeric**

1 teaspoon **ground cumin**

1 teaspoon **ground coriander**

2 tablespoons **freshly squeezed lemon juice** (½ lemon), or more to taste

3 tablespoons **very finely chopped fresh cilantro**

2 tablespoons **all-purpose flour**

salt and **freshly ground black pepper**

Raita (see pages 163–164) or **Cilantro** or **Tamarind Chutney** (see pages 215 and 217), to serve

Delicately spiced potato cakes—excellent as a side dish and perfect for parties. Try adding defrosted frozen peas to the mix, too.

Cook the potatoes in boiling salted water for about 10 minutes, until only just tender. Drain and spread out in a colander to steam dry; this will ensure your patties are firm not squishy. When cool enough to handle, chop into smaller pieces, then place in a bowl and roughly mash—it doesn't need to be smooth (we keep the skins in the mix).

Heat the oil in a small skillet over a medium heat. Add the mustard seeds and, when they start to crackle, add the onion and a pinch of salt. Cook for about 8 minutes, stirring, until the onion begins to brown. Reduce the heat, add the garlic, ginger, chili pepper, and ground spices and cook for 2 minutes, stirring. Stir this mixture into the potatoes, along with the lemon juice, cilantro, flour, and some black pepper. Taste and add more salt or lemon juice, if needed—it should be very well seasoned.

Chill the mixture in the fridge for 1 hour (or in the freezer for 20 minutes).

Pour a layer of flour onto a plate and season well. Pour a 1-inch depth of oil or ghee (or a mixture) into a large skillet and set over a high heat until shimmering hot.

Shape mashed potatoes into the size of ping-pong balls, then roll them in the flour and gently squash flat with your palm, until about 1½ inches wide and ¾ inch thick. Dust off excess flour and carefully slide the patties into the hot oil. Cook for about 2 minutes on each side, until golden and crisp on the bottoms, then flip and repeat. Remove to drain on paper towel and keep warm while you cook the rest.

Serve hot, with raita or cilantro or tamarind chutney.

PEA & POTATO SAMOSAS

MAKES 16

PREP TIME: 35 MINS • COOK TIME: 50 MINS

DF • V • VE • NF • SoF • SUITABLE FOR FREEZING

neutral cooking oil, for frying

Coconut Chutney (see page 217) and
  Tamarind Yogurt (see page 165),
  to serve

FOR THE PASTRY:

6 ounces **all-purpose flour**, plus extra for
  dusting

¼ teaspoon **salt**

1½ tablespoons **neutral cooking oil**

FOR THE FILLING:

1 pound **white potatoes**, peeled and diced

7 ounces (1 large) **carrot**, peeled and diced

1 tablespoon **neutral cooking oil**, plus
  extra as needed

1 **onion**, finely diced

2 cloves of **garlic**, grated

1½-inch piece of **ginger**, peeled and grated

½ teaspoon **ground turmeric**

½ teaspoon **crushed red pepper** (optional)

1 teaspoon **garam masala**

1 teaspoon **mustard seeds**

3 ounces **frozen peas**

2 tablespoons **finely chopped fresh
  cilantro**

1 teaspoon **lemon juice**

salt and **freshly ground black pepper**

We developed this version of the classic samosa for our book, **Fast
Vegan.** *We like it so much we decided to include it here, too.*

First, make the pastry. Combine the flour and salt in a bowl, then rub in the oil with your fingers. When the mixture is sandy, add enough water (3–4 tablespoons) to form a dough. You may not need it all, as the dough should not be sticky. When the dough is still quite dry and craggy, knead for up to 5 minutes, until smooth and elastic. Place the ball of dough into a clean bowl, cover with plastic wrap or a dish towel, and set aside to rest while you make the filling.

Cook the potatoes and carrot in a large saucepan of salted boiling water for about 15 minutes, until tender.

Meanwhile, heat the oil in a skillet over a medium heat. When hot, add the onion and a pinch of salt and sauté for about 8 minutes, until translucent and beginning to brown. Add the garlic and ginger and cook, stirring, for 1 minute. Add the turmeric, crushed red pepper, if using, garam masala, and mustard seeds, plus another splash of oil if the pan seems dry. Cook for 1 minute, then remove from the heat. Add the frozen peas and cilantro leaves, stir, and set aside.

Drain the potatoes and carrot, then roughly mash, leaving some chunks for texture. Stir in the contents of the onion pan, along with the lemon juice and some black pepper. Taste and add more salt, if needed.

RECIPE CONTINUES ➝

Set a deep skillet over a medium heat and pour in a 1½-inch depth of cooking oil. Heat to 350°F (if you have a deep-fry thermometer), or until a cube of day-old bread fizzes and browns in 30 seconds.

Meanwhile, divide the pastry dough into 8 pieces, then shape into neat balls. Dust a work surface and rolling pin with flour, then roll out one ball to a very thin circle of pastry, about 8 inches across. Use a sharp knife to halve the circle. Shape the semicircle of pastry into a cone by folding it over on itself, one-third at a time. Wet the outer edge of the pastry and thoroughly seal it like a seam, pinching it firmly shut at the bottom of the cone so that the filling doesn't leak when frying.

To fill, make a circle with your thumb and forefinger and use it to support the open-topped cone. Use a spoon to fill the cone about three-quarters full, then wet the remaining open edges and pinch firmly shut.

Repeat until all the pastry is used up.

Fry 2 or 3 samosas at a time, for 2–3 minutes on each side, until golden brown and bubbly all over. Use a slotted spoon or tongs to remove them from the pan, draining any excess oil back into the pan. Set to drain on a plate lined with paper towel and keep warm while you cook the rest.

Serve hot, with coconut chutney and tamarind yogurt, plus some Indian pickles.

=== TIP ===

To reheat, defrost if frozen, then place in the oven at 400°F for 8–10 minutes.

RAITA

2 teaspoons **neutral cooking oil**

½ teaspoon **black mustard seeds**

3 ounces (approx. 5-inch piece) **cucumber**, deseeded and finely diced

3 ounces (1 small) **carrot**, very finely diced (optional)

8 heaped tablespoons **thick whole-milk plain yogurt** (can be nondairy)

leaves from 1 bushy sprig of **mint**, finely chopped

a pinch of **sea salt**, or to taste

a small pinch of **sugar** (optional)

We have included twelve different kinds of raita in this book. We're obsessed.

Heat the oil in a small saucepan set over a medium heat. When hot, add the mustard seeds and as soon as they start to pop, remove from the heat.

Place the cucumber, carrot (if using), yogurt, mint leaves, salt, and mustards seeds (leaving most of the oil behind) in a bowl. Mix, then taste and decide if you want to add sugar or more salt.

Set aside until ready to serve. This will keep for 1–2 days, covered, in the fridge.

There are so many variations! Add finely diced shallot; ground cumin, toasted briefly after cooking the mustard seeds; 4–5 cherry tomatoes, deseeded and very finely chopped; a good pinch of chili powder; chaat masala spice mix; or leftover cooked vegetables, finely chopped, such as eggplant, okra, green beans, cabbage, or cauliflower. Yum.

RINKU'S POMEGRANATE & CILANTRO RAITA

SERVES 4 AS A SIDE

PREP TIME: 15 MINS, PLUS 1 HOUR CHILLING • COOK TIME: 1 MIN

WF • GF • DF • V • Ve (if substituting the yogurt) • **NF • SoF** (unless using nut or soy yogurt)

1 tablespoon **cumin seeds**

1 large **pomegranate**

1¾ cups **whole-milk plain yogurt** (can be nondairy)

a handful of **fresh cilantro**, finely chopped

a handful of **fresh mint**, finely chopped

1 teaspoon **black salt** (or a generous pinch of **sea salt**, if preferred)

2 tablespoons **freshly squeezed lime juice**

1 tablespoon **brown sugar**

¼ teaspoon **freshly ground black pepper**

¼ teaspoon **chili powder** (optional)

≡ TIP ≡

Any leftover pomegranate seeds will make a lovely garnish for almost any curry in this book—at LEON, we use them in wraps and over mezze-style salads. They are rich in antioxidants and release a juicy burst of tanginess when you pop them in your mouth.

A crunchy and cooling side for spicy mains (or barbecued meats or grilled fish). If you love the sauce in the LEON lamb kofte wrap, you will love this—try it with the Lamb Keema on page 145.

Place a small skillet over a medium heat. Dry-roast the cumin seeds until fragrant, taking care not to burn them. Remove from the heat and allow to cool, then grind to a fine powder.

Cut the pomegranate in half and tap the top gently with a tablespoon over a bowl— the seeds should gently loosen and fall out. Take the remaining seeds out by hand, ensuring no white pith comes with them.

Mix all of the ingredients in a large bowl, reserving about 1 tablespoon of pomegranate seeds and a good pinch of the chopped cilantro leaves, for garnish. Cover and place the bowl in the fridge for at least 1 hour, to allow the flavors to develop.

Take the raita out of the fridge 30 minutes before serving, to allow it to reach room temperature. Give it a final stir, and garnish with the reserved pomegranate seeds and cilantro.

TAMARIND YOGURT

SERVES 4
PREP TIME: 5 MINS
WF • GF • V • DF • Ve (if substituting the yogurt) • **NF • SoF** (unless using nut or soy yogurt)

2 teaspoons **tamarind paste** or
  concentrate
½ cup **whole-milk plain yogurt** (can be
  nondairy)
2 teaspoons **finely chopped fresh mint**
a pinch of **ground cumin**
a pinch of **salt**

For dipping, drizzling, and dolloping.

Stir all the ingredients together, then taste and add more salt, as needed.

RINKU'S BEET PACHADI

SERVES 4 AS A SIDE
PREP TIME: 8 MINS • COOK TIME: 2 MINS
WF • GF • DF • V • Ve (if substituting the yogurt) • **NF • SoF** (unless using nut or soy yogurt)

3 medium **pre-cooked beets** (not in vinegar), chopped into ¾-inch chunks

¾ cup **whole-milk plain yogurt** (can be nondairy)

1 ounce **desiccated coconut**

2 **green chili peppers** (deseeded or not, to taste)

¾-inch piece of **ginger**, peeled and finely grated

salt, to taste

water, as required

1 tablespoon **rapeseed oil**

1 teaspoon **black mustard seeds**

1 tablespoon **curry leaves**

≡ TIP ≡

If cooking the beets yourself from scratch, wash, then wrap each one in foil. Roast for about 45 minutes at 350°F, or until tender to the point of a knife. Cool, then rub off the skins with your thumbs.

Rebecca would like to thank her friend Rinku for patiently teaching her all sorts of curry lore and wisdom. And for feeding her. "Pachadi is from Kerala and Tamil Nadu. The base is coconut and yogurt, and seasonal vegetables are then added. In our home, it is very popular, I think because of the gorgeous color."

Place the beets, yogurt, coconut, chili peppers, ginger, and a pinch of salt into a blender or food processor. Add very little water to begin with and briefly blitz, adding more water as necessary to help it come together. We like to have a few bits of beet that haven't been completely blended in, so usually two 15-second blitzes will do the trick. Taste for salt and add as needed. Transfer the mixture to a nice serving bowl.

Heat the oil in a small saucepan over a medium heat. When hot, add the black mustard seeds and the curry leaves, and cook for 15 seconds, or until the curry leaves are aromatic. Remove from the heat, pour this mixture over the pachadi mixture, and serve.

RICE

COCONUT RICE

SERVES 4
PREP TIME: 5 MINS • COOK TIME: 11
MINS, PLUS 10 MINS STANDING
WF • GF • DF • V • Ve • NF • SoF

9 ounces **uncooked jasmine rice**
1¼ cups **coconut milk** (from a well-shaken can)
a pinch of **salt**

This rice is excellent with fiercely spicy dishes, and most South Asian curries. Light coconut milk is liable to separate, so make sure you use a good-quality full-fat type.

Rinse the rice well under cold running water. Tip into a saucepan with a lid, then mix in 1 cup water, the coconut milk, and salt. Bring to a boil, then reduce the heat, cover, and simmer for 11 minutes.

Remove from the heat, take the lid off, and fluff up the grains of rice with a fork. Replace the lid and leave to steam for 10 minutes, then serve.

CURD RICE

SERVES 4
PREP TIME: 10 MINS • COOK TIME: 2 MINS
WF • GF • V • DF • NF • SoF

1½ pounds **freshly cooked basmati rice** (or 9 ounces **uncooked rice**, steamed)
1 tablespoon **neutral cooking oil**
½ teaspoon each **mustard** and **cumin seeds**
5 **curry leaves**, torn into little pieces
1 **green chili pepper**, deseeded and finely chopped (optional)
½ teaspoon **asafetida**
4 heaped tablespoons **whole-milk plain yogurt**
a handful of **fresh cilantro**, to garnish
2 tablespoons **pomegranate seeds**, to serve

A soothing mellow rice, made with yogurt.

Set the freshly cooked rice aside to cool to warm, as very hot rice may make the yogurt separate.

Heat the oil in a small skillet set over a medium heat. Add the mustard seeds and, when they start to pop, add the cumin seeds, curry leaves, and chili pepper, if using. Sizzle for 1 minute, then remove from the heat and add the asafetida.

Spoon the yogurt into the warm rice and mix well, then add the tempered spices and the oil from the pan. Mix well and serve immediately, topped with the cilantro leaves and pomegranate seeds (or chill completely, immediately, and eat cold—but do not keep for more than 24 hours).

BLACK RICE

SERVES 4
PREP TIME: 1 MIN • COOK TIME: 45–50
MINS, PLUS 10 MINS STANDING
WF • GF • DF • V • Ve • NF • SoF

9 ounces **black/forbidden rice**

5 cups **water**

a generous pinch of **salt**

≡ TIP ≡

If you can't find black rice, look for red rice, or mixed basmati and wild rice, as a change from white rice.

Nutty and with lots of bite, black rice is a very nutritious alternative to the white stuff. (We are also fans of brown rice at LEON and we've a lot of time for quinoa, too.) Whether or not to rinse and soak black rice is up for debate—some reckon doing both means that good antioxidants are lost, while others say it cooks more quickly and is less sticky if you do. What isn't in question, though, is that those anthocyanins that make it so good for us will stain anything they can—clothes, ceramic or enamel pans, and work surfaces—so be careful.

Place everything in a saucepan with a well-fitting lid and bring to a simmer over a medium heat. Reduce the heat to low, cover, and cook for 45–50 minutes, stirring once or twice so it doesn't stick to the bottom of the pan, until the rice is tender but with a little bite.

Remove from the heat, fluff the rice grains up with a fork, then cover again and leave to stand for 10 minutes or so, before serving.

JEERA RICE

SERVES 4
PREP TIME: 5 MINS, PLUS 30 MINS SOAKING
COOK TIME: 14 MINS, PLUS 10 MINS
STANDING
WF • GF • DF • V • Ve • NF • SoF

9 ounces **basmati rice**

2 tablespoons **neutral cooking oil**

1 teaspoon **cumin seeds**

a pinch of **salt**

Fragrant, earthy rice flavored with cumin seeds (aka jeera).

Rinse the rice well under cold running water. Place in a bowl, cover with cold water, and leave to soak for up to 30 minutes. Drain.

Heat the oil in a large saucepan with a lid, set over a medium heat. When hot, add the cumin seeds and toast for 30 seconds. Add the rice and toss for 1–2 minutes, letting the oil coat the grains of rice. Add 2 cups water and the salt, cover, and bring to a boil. Reduce the heat to low and simmer for 12 minutes.

Remove the lid, fluff up the grains of rice with a fork, then replace the lid and leave to steam for a further 5–10 minutes.

5 WAYS WITH CAULIFLOWER RICE

SERVES 4
PREP TIME: 5 MINS • COOK TIME: 7 MINS, PLUS 3–4 MINS STANDING
WF • GF • DF • V • VE • NF • SoF

1¼ pounds **cauliflower florets**
2 teaspoons **neutral cooking oil**
salt

A low-carb substitute for traditional rice, we were happily surprised by how well this works when we first tried making it.

Place some of the cauliflower florets into the bowl of a food processor, filling it no more than halfway. Whizz for 15–20 seconds—you want grains about the size of small couscous, but no finer, or the "rice" will be mushy when cooked. If larger pieces remain, tip everything into a bowl, pick out the big bits, and process them on their own. Repeat until all the cauliflower is couscous-like.

To cook, use the widest skillet you have, so that the cauliflower cooks in the thinnest possible layer. Set the pan over a medium-low heat and add the oil, then tip the cauliflower into the pan and spread out in a thin, even layer. Let it cook for 1–2 minutes, then use a heat-resistant spatula to shimmy it around the pan, then rearrange in a thin layer again. Repeat this process 3 times, letting the cauliflower become golden in places.

Remove from the heat, stir, and leave in the hot pan for 3–4 minutes, so that even more moisture can evaporate. Serve as it is, seasoned with a little salt, as needed.

≡ VARIATIONS ≡

FOR SOUTH ASIAN OR JAPANESE DISHES: Cook as here, then add a splash of **soy sauce**, a handful of chopped **scallions**, and ½ teaspoon peeled and finely grated **ginger** or a dash of **sesame oil**. Mix very well before serving.

FOR THAI DISHES: Cook as here, then dress to taste with a little **fish sauce** and freshly squeezed **lime juice**, off the heat. (Add ½ teaspoon of each to begin with.)

FOR INDIAN DISHES: Before cooking the cauliflower, and in the same pan and oil, toast a pinch of **mustard seeds** until they pop, then add a pinch of **cumin seeds**, 1 crushed clove of **garlic**, and ¼ teaspoon **ground turmeric**. Cook for 1 minute, before adding the **cauliflower**, then cook as here.

FOR COCONUT STICKY "RICE": Cook as here, then dress with 1–2 tablespoons **coconut milk** and a pinch of **salt**.

≡ TIP ≡

The outer leaves and stem of the cauliflower can be saved and added to slaw, finely sliced. Cool any leftover cauliflower rice and refrigerate immediately, then use within 24 hours in place of couscous in salads.

3 WAYS WITH FRIED RICE

EGG-FRIED RICE WITH SOY SAUCE

SERVES 2 AS A MAIN OR 4 AS A SIDE
PREP TIME: 10 MINS • COOK TIME: 8 MINS
WF • GF (check tamari/soy sauce ingredients) • DF • V • Ve (without egg)

1 tablespoon **neutral cooking oil**

2 cloves of **garlic**, finely sliced (optional)

1 **scallion**, white and green parts divided, finely diced

12 ounces **cooked Japanese short-grain rice** or **jasmine rice** (or 5 ounces **uncooked rice**, cooked)

1 tablespoon **tamari/soy sauce**

1 **egg**, lightly beaten (optional, but recommended)

lime wedges, to serve

This is Japanese-style fried rice, but you can also serve it with Chinese-style recipes. It's a great way to use up leftovers and is soothing—great for colds, flu or hangovers. (Not that we ever have those. Not us.)

Heat the oil in a large skillet or wok set over a medium-high heat. When hot, add the garlic and white parts of the scallion and cook for 2 minutes, stirring, until the garlic begins to brown. Add the rice and sprinkle over the tamari/soy sauce, tossing so that it coats the rice evenly, and breaking up any lumps. After 2 minutes, push the rice to the side and add the egg to the pan, if using. Allow it to cook for about 1 minute, moving it around so that it scrambles lightly, then stir it into the rice.

Remove from the heat and serve immediately, sprinkled with the remaining scallion.

≡ TIP ≡
Finish with a pinch of sesame seeds, if you like.

INDIAN-STYLE FRIED RICE

SERVES 2 AS A MAIN OR 4 AS A SIDE
PREP TIME: 15 MINS • COOK TIME: 8 MINS
WF • GF • DF • V • VE • NF • SoF

1 tablespoon **neutral cooking oil**

½ teaspoon **mustard seeds**

4–5 **curry leaves**

½ teaspoon **cumin seeds**

2 **scallions**, finely chopped

1–2 cloves of **garlic**, crushed, to taste,

¾-inch piece of **ginger**, peeled and finely grated

½ teaspoon **ground turmeric**

12 ounces **cooked leftover basmati rice** (or 5 ounces **uncooked rice**, cooked)

a handful of **fresh cilantro leaves**, chopped

freshly squeezed lemon juice

salt and **freshly ground black pepper**

Rice with tempered seeds and fresh herbs—wonderful on its own or with leftover curry.

Heat the oil in a large skillet or wok set over a medium heat. When hot, add the mustard seeds and, when they start to pop, add the curry leaves and cumin seeds. When the cumin is fragrant, add the scallions, garlic, and ginger, and stir-fry for 1 minute or so. Add the turmeric and then the rice, and stir-fry until the rice is piping hot and bright yellow throughout.

Remove from the heat and add the cilantro leaves, a splash of lemon juice, and plenty of salt and pepper. Toss well again, then serve immediately.

═ TIP ═

Be sure to chill your leftover rice immediately, and store for no more than 24 hours, otherwise it can be home to some pretty nasty bugs.

THAI-STYLE FRIED RICE

SERVES 2 AS A MAIN OR 4 AS A SIDE
PREP TIME: 10 MINS • COOK TIME: 6 MINS
WF • GF • DF • V • VE (if substituting fish sauce and nam prik pao) • SoF

1 tablespoon **neutral cooking oil**

1 clove of **garlic**, crushed

3 tablespoons chopped **unroasted peanuts** or **cashews** (optional)

2 **scallions**, finely sliced

1 **red chili pepper** (deseeded or not, to taste), finely chopped

12 ounces **cooked leftover jasmine rice** (or 5 ounces **uncooked rice**, cooked)

2 teaspoons **fish sauce**, plus extra as needed (vegetarians and vegans can omit and add **salt** instead, or a pinch of **seaweed powder**)

7 ounces **Asian greens**, shredded

freshly squeezed lime juice

Sriracha hot sauce or **nam prik pao**, or similar **Thai** or **Asian chili paste/oil**, to serve

═ TIP ═
Add in and stir-fry some seafood, leftover cooked pork or chicken, or egg (or add a fried egg to serve). Finish with Thai basil or fresh cilantro.

This was a new discovery for us. And it's one we're so happy to have made.

Heat the oil in a large skillet or wok set over a medium-high heat. When hot, add the garlic, nuts, if using, scallions, and chili pepper, and sizzle for 1 minute. Add the rice, fish sauce, and greens and stir-fry for 3–4 minutes, until the greens are just wilted.

Remove from the heat and squeeze over the lime juice. Drizzle with Sriracha or chili paste/oil, then toss and taste. Serve immediately.

TIP

Pilau can be made plain by omitting the meat or vegetarian/vegan by swapping the meat for mixed vegetables (fresh or frozen diced carrots, corn, and green beans work well); in which case, omit the 50–60 minutes stove-top cooking in the first step.

SHUMAIYA'S AKHNI PILAU

SERVES 8–10

PREP TIME: 20 MINS • COOK TIME: 1 HOUR 50 MINS

WF • GF • DF (if using oil or nondairy ghee) **• NF • SoF**

3–4 tablespoons **neutral cooking oil** or **ghee**

3 **onions**, finely chopped

2-inch piece of **ginger**, peeled and finely grated

4 cloves of **garlic**, crushed

1 teaspoon **cumin seeds**

2-inch stick of **cinnamon**, broken into large pieces

3 **bay leaves**

4 **green cardamom pods**

2¼ pounds **beef** or **lamb**, ideally bone-in, cut into 1–1½-inch chunks

2 teaspoons **salt**

4–5 **green bird's-eye chili peppers**, sliced lengthways (or less, or omit, to taste)

1 teaspoon **ground coriander**

1½ teaspoons **garam masala**

2½ cups **hot water**

14 ounces **uncooked basmati rice**

½ teaspoon **ground cinnamon**

finely sliced **red** or **green chili pepper**, to serve (optional)

Our friend Shumi is from a Bengali family. "This meat pilau is usually served up for special occasions or when guests come to visit. It's made with aromatic spices, so the rice doesn't clash with whatever curry it's being served with." Serve with a lamb, beef, chicken or vegetable curry, with an onion salad on the side (try the Kachumber Salad on page 192).

Heat enough oil or ghee to cover the base of a large heavy saucepan with a lid, set over a medium heat. Add half each of the onions, ginger, and garlic, and cook until golden. Add the cumin seeds, cinnamon, bay leaves, cardamom pods, meat, and salt. Stir to combine, then reduce the heat, cover, and let the meat stew in its own juices for 50–60 minutes, ensuring it doesn't dry up. Add a dash or two of water, if needed, and stir every 5–10 minutes. Heat the oven to 325°F.

When the meat is tender, set a separate large ovenproof saucepan with a lid over a low-medium heat, and add the remaining ghee and onions. Cook for about 8 minutes, until the onions start to soften, then add the remaining ginger and garlic, along with the bird's-eye chili peppers. Cook for 5 minutes, stirring occasionally. Add the ground coriander and 1 teaspoon of the garam masala, and cook for another 5 minutes, until the oil separates from the onions.

Add the cooked meat mixture to the ovenproof pan, along with its juices, and bring to a boil. Pour in the hot water, then add the rice, ground cinnamon, and remaining garam masala, and stir everything together. Cover and bake in the oven for 25–30 minutes, until all the liquid has been absorbed and the surface looks slightly dry.

Remove from the oven and let stand, with the lid on, for 5 minutes. Serve immediately, garnished with chili peppers.

COCONUT RICE 'N' PEAS

9 ounces **uncooked basmati rice**

1 cup **coconut milk**

14 ounces **canned kidney beans**, **black beans**, or **pigeon peas** (or a can containing a mix of all 3 beans), drain and reserve the water (see below)

1 cup **water** (use the water from the bean can, topped up with more water if needed)

1 **scallion**, finely chopped

1 medium **red chili pepper**, slit down one side

1 sprig **fresh thyme** or a tiny pinch of **dried thyme**

salt (optional) and **freshly ground black pepper**

Serve this with the Heartbreak Curry (see page 38), or any Caribbean-style curry.

Wash the rice under cold running water and set aside.

In a large saucepan with a lid, mix together the coconut milk, beans, measured bean water/water, scallion, chili pepper, thyme, a pinch of salt (unless the bean water was already salted), and some black pepper. Bring to a simmer, then add the washed rice. Cover and cook for 12 minutes, stirring once or twice towards the end of cooking.

Remove from the heat and leave to stand, still covered with a lid, for 5–8 minutes. Fluff up with a fork before serving.

≡ TIP ≡

Some recipes recommend using a whole Scotch bonnet, rather than an ordinary chili pepper– this makes the rice very spicy, but go for it, if you're brave.

CRISPY ONIONS

SERVES 4 AS A TOPPING
PREP TIME: 5 MINS • COOK TIME: 30–35 MINS
WF • GF • DF • V • VE • NF • SoF

3 tablespoons **neutral cooking oil**

2 **onions**, finely sliced into half moons

a pinch of **salt**

There's almost no curry that won't benefit from a handful of crispy onions, especially lentil curries and anything vegan. Take your time over this one—rushing equals burnt and bitter onions. (P.S. You can buy these ready made...)

Heat the oil in a wide skillet set over the lowest heat possible. Add the onions and cook really slowly for up to 35 minutes, stirring often, until deep brown, nutty, sweet, and really crisp.

Lift out with a slotted spoon and drain off any excess oil on paper towel. Toss with a little pinch of salt before using.

≡ TIP ≡

Once cooled, these will keep in a sealed container for 4–5 days. Crisp up in a hot skillet before using, if necessary.

STEAMED GREENS

SERVES 4
PREP TIME: 10 MINS • COOK TIME: 10 MINS
DF • WF • GF (check soy sauce ingredients, if using) • V • Ve (if substituting fish sauce) • NF

a splash of **neutral cooking oil**

1 pound **shredded bok choy** or other **mild Asian greens**, or **broccolini**, **Chinese long beans**, **snow peas**, **sugar-snap peas**, freshly washed and still wet

FOR THAI/VIETNAMESE STYLE:

a pinch of **salt**

1 clove of **garlic**, peeled and bruised

1 tablespoon **fish sauce** (vegetarians/vegans can substitute **soy sauce**)

1 tablespoon **freshly squeezed lime juice** (omit if using soy sauce)

a pinch of **black** or **white sesame seeds**

FOR INDIAN-STYLE:

½ **onion**, chopped

1 clove of **garlic**, crushed

1 teaspoon peeled and finely grated **ginger**

½ teaspoon **cumin seeds**

½ teaspoon **mustard seeds**

½ **green chili pepper**, finely chopped

1 tablespoon **dessicated coconut** (optional)

salt and **freshly ground black pepper**

freshly squeezed lemon juice, to serve

Greens are at the heart of what we do at LEON (our New Original Salad has been a bestseller for 15 years now), and we know that—done right—they can be so good that nobody will need nudging to eat them. Tweak the seasonings, as below, and these sautéed greens will go with either Indian-style or Southeast Asian-style curries.

FOR THAI/VIETNAMESE-STYLE GREENS:

Heat the oil in a large skillet with a lid, set over a medium heat. Add the wet greens or vegetables, salt, and garlic (plus a couple of extra tablespoons of water, if the pan seems dry). Cover with a lid and steam for 3–4 minutes, then remove the lid and stir everything a couple of times. If the vegetables need a little more cooking, return the lid to the pan and cook for 1–2 minutes longer, otherwise remove from the heat. Mix together the fish sauce and lime juice (or just use soy sauce), and dress the cooked greens. Sprinkle with black or white sesame seeds before serving.

FOR INDIAN-STYLE GREENS:

Heat the oil in a large skillet, set over a medium heat. Add the onion and sauté for 5 minutes, then add the garlic, ginger, cumin seeds, mustard seeds, and green chili pepper. (If serving with something coconutty, add the desiccated coconut at the same time as the spices.) Cook for 5 minutes, until the mustard seeds crackle, then add the greens or vegetables, along with a pinch of salt and pepper. Sauté until the greens are just wilted, or the vegetables are tender, less than 5 minutes. Squeeze over a little lemon juice before serving.

≡ TIP ≡

Use the method for
Indian-style greens as a way
of using up leftover cooked
vegetables (or frozen vegetables),
such as carrots, eggplant, potatoes,
peas, corn, cabbage, or even
Brussels sprouts.

CABBAGE, PEA, & POTATO CURRY

SERVES 2 AS A MAIN OR 4 AS A SIDE
PREP TIME: 15 MINS • COOK TIME: 15 MINS
WF • GF • DF • V • Ve • NF • SoF

1 tablespoon **neutral cooking oil**

½ teaspoon **mustard seeds**

¼ teaspoon **cumin seeds**

½ teaspoon **asafetida**

½ teaspoon **ground turmeric**

4 **curry leaves**

½–1 **green chili pepper** (deseeded or not, to taste), finely chopped

½ teaspoon **ground coriander**

10 ounces **cabbage**, core and ribs removed, finely shredded

9 ounces **potatoes**, peeled and cut into ½-inch chunks

4 tablespoons **water**

4 ounces **frozen peas**

about 2 teaspoons **freshly squeezed lemon** or **lime juice**, to serve (optional)

salt and **freshly ground black pepper**

═ TIP ═

Leftovers are great in Curry Wraps (see page 211). This is also good with cauliflower, broken into little florets, either instead of the cabbage or potatoes, or as an extra ingredient.

We love to use sweet green cabbage, such as napa, here, but any cabbage will work beautifully. If you don't have any asafetida powder (find it in the spice aisle of a specialty supermarket), use a crushed clove of garlic, or a pinch of onion or garlic powder, instead.

Heat the oil in a large saucepan with a lid set over a medium heat. Add the mustard seeds and, when they start to crackle, add the cumin seeds. Sizzle for 30 seconds, then quickly add the asafetida, turmeric, curry leaves, green chili pepper, and coriander. Mix well, letting them cook for no more than 30 seconds, then add the cabbage, potatoes, and water, plus a good dose of salt and pepper. Toss well, then reduce the heat to low, cover with the lid, and cook for 10 minutes, or until the potatoes are tender.

Add the peas to the pan, mix well again, then cook for a final 2 minutes. (You shouldn't need to, but if there's a lot of liquid, remove the lid and increase the heat to bubble away any excess.) Squeeze over the lemon or lime juice, if using, then taste to check for salt, pepper, and lemon levels, adding more as needed.

Serve immediately, as a side dish or as a light main with raita (see pages 163–4) or plain yogurt, Lime Pickle (see page 214), Mango Chutney (see page 216), and flatbreads, such as roti/chapati (see page 200).

BEET THORAN

SERVES 4 AS A MAIN OR SIDE
PREP TIME: 15 MINS • COOK TIME: 20–27 MINS
WF • GF • DF • V • Ve • NF • SoF

1 tablespoon **neutral cooking oil**

2 teaspoons **mustard seeds**

½ teaspoon **cumin seeds**

3 ounces **shallots**, finely sliced

5 **curry leaves**, torn

½ teaspoon **ground turmeric**

1 pound **beets**, washed, peeled, and finely grated (see tip)

3 tablespoons **desiccated coconut**

3 tablespoons **hot water**

salt

This dry, curried vegetable dish from south India can be made with almost any shreddable root vegetable, or you could use shredded cabbage, Chinese long beans, canned unripe green jackfruit, or greens, such as spinach.

Heat the oil in a large wide saucepan with a lid set over a medium heat. When hot, add the mustard seeds and, when they start to crackle and pop, add the cumin seeds and cook for 1–2 minutes, until fragrant. Reduce the heat to low, add the shallots and curry leaves, along with a pinch of salt, and cook for 5 minutes, until the shallots have softened a little.

Add the turmeric and then the grated beets and desiccated coconut, and stir-fry gently for 3–4 minutes. Finally, add the water, cover with a lid, and cook gently for 10–15 minutes, stirring once or twice, until the beets are tender but still have some bite.

Serve hot, as a side, or with rice or flatbreads (see pages 198–201 and 205–206) and raita (see pages 163–164) as a light lunch.

≡ **TIP** ≡

Use the grater attachment on a food processor, if you have one, or wear gloves, if you don't want pink fingers.

BOMBAY POTATOES

SERVES 4 AS A SIDE
PREP TIME: 10 MINS • COOK TIME: 20 MINS
WF • GF • DF • V • Ve • NF • SoF • SUITABLE FOR FREEZING

1 pound **new** or **baby potatoes**, cut into small chunks

1 tablespoon **neutral cooking oil**

½ teaspoon **mustard seeds**

½ teaspoon **cumin seeds**

1 clove of **garlic**, crushed

¾-inch piece of **ginger**, peeled and grated

2 teaspoons **tomato paste**

¼ teaspoon **ground turmeric**

salt

freshly squeezed lemon juice, to serve

This is the very easiest version of Bombay potatoes—if you have a little more time, start by softening an onion in the oil, before adding the garlic, ginger and spices.

Simmer the potatoes in a saucepan of boiling salted water for 12–17 minutes, until tender. Drain.

Towards the end of the potatoes' cooking time, heat the oil in a skillet over a medium heat. Add the mustard seeds and, when they start to pop, add the cumin seeds, reduce the heat to low, and cook for 1 minute. Add the garlic, ginger, tomato paste, and turmeric, and cook for 2–3 minutes, until fragrant. Add the potatoes to the pan along with 2 tablespoons of water, just enough to loosen the sauce so that it coats the potatoes.

Sauté the potatoes gently, stirring and tossing until hot through and evenly covered in the spiced sauce. Remove from the heat. Sprinkle with a pinch of salt and a squeeze of lemon, stir once again, and then serve.

≡ TIP ≡

If you have some, frizzle 3 or 4 torn curry leaves in the hot oil, when you add the cumin seeds.

BAKED ALOO GOBI

SERVES 4
PREP TIME: 15 MINS • COOK TIME: 45 MINS
WF • GF • DF • V • Ve • NF • SoF

3 tablespoons **neutral cooking oil**

1 pound **potatoes**, unpeeled, cut into
¾–1-inch chunks

2 **onions**, each cut into 6–8 wedges

2 cloves of **garlic**, crushed

1-inch piece of **ginger**, peeled and finely
grated

¼–½ teaspoon **chili powder**,
to taste

½ teaspoon **nigella seeds** (optional)

1 teaspoon **cumin seeds**

1 teaspoon **coriander seeds**

1 teaspoon **tomato paste**

1 small **cauliflower**, chopped into small
¾–1-inch florets

7 ounces **canned diced tomatoes** or
fresh tomatoes, chopped

1 cup **hot water**

salt and **freshly ground black pepper**

freshly squeezed lemon juice, to serve

a handful of **fresh cilantro**, roughly
chopped

≡ TIP ≡

Any leftovers? Turn to page 211 and use
them in one of our curry wraps.

We do love curries where all you need to do is chuck it all in a tray.

Heat the oven to 375°F.

Choose a large, ideally metal, baking dish or roasting tray that will allow all the ingredients to fit in a single layer. Pour in the oil, then add the potatoes and onions. Toss well, then arrange in a single layer. Bake in the oven for 10 minutes.

Remove from the oven and add a dusting of black pepper and a generous pinch of salt, plus the garlic, ginger, chili powder, nigella seeds, if using, cumin seeds, coriander seeds, tomato paste, cauliflower florets, and fresh tomatoes, if using. Toss well, then return to the oven for 20 minutes, stirring once halfway through.

Remove from the oven and mix in the canned tomatoes, if using, and water, then bake for a final 15 minutes, until the potatoes are cooked through and the cauliflower is tender. If it seems watery, don't worry, just give it a good stir to allow the water to incorporate into the tomato-y sauce.

Squeeze over a little lemon juice and stir through half of the cilantro. Taste and add more salt, pepper, or lemon juice, as needed. Finish with the last of the cilantro and serve immediately.

KOSHAMBARI SALAD

SERVES 4 AS A SIDE
PREP TIME: 10 MINS • COOK TIME: 30 MINS
WF • GF • DF • V • Ve • SoF

5 ounces **yellow mung/moong dal** (also known as split huskless mung beans), rinsed

1 tablespoon **neutral cooking oil**

2 teaspoons **mustard seeds**

8 **curry leaves**, roughly torn

2 tablespoons **desiccated coconut**

2 ounces **unroasted peanuts** or **cashews**, pummelled or chopped into small pieces (optional)

4 ounces **cucumber**, finely diced

a handful of **fresh cilantro**, roughly chopped

freshly squeezed lemon juice

salt

This nutty lentil salad is very moreish. In the southern states of India it is made with raw split mung beans, soaked for a few hours, but we are a bit wary of eating raw pulses, so prefer to simmer ours for half an hour first.

Place the yellow mung dal in a saucepan, cover with fresh cold water, and bring to a brisk boil. Reduce the heat and simmer for 30 minutes, until tender but not falling apart, skimming off any scum that rises to the surface.

Meanwhile, heat the oil in a small skillet over a medium heat. Add the mustard seeds and, when they start to pop, add the curry leaves, coconut, and nuts, and cook for 2–3 minutes, stirring constantly, just until the coconut and nuts are golden brown—don't let them burn. Remove from the heat and tip the mixture straight into a serving bowl.

Drain the lentils, then cool under cold running water. Add to the bowl, along with the cucumber, cilantro leaves, and a little squeeze of lemon. Add a small pinch of salt, then toss and taste, adding more salt or lemon as needed. Serve immediately.

═ TIP ═

You can make this with or without the lentils, and grated raw beets or carrot is a delicious addition, as is a dollop of plain yogurt as a dressing. Spice it up by adding finely chopped green chili pepper when you crackle the mustard seeds.

KACHUMBER SALAD

SERVES 4 AS A RELISH
PREP TIME: 10 MINS, PLUS 10 MINS STANDING
WF • GF • DF • V • Ve • NF • SoF

1 ounce **shallots**, finely chopped

3 ounces **cherry tomatoes**, finely chopped

2 ounces **cucumber**, finely chopped

freshly squeezed lemon juice

salt

a handful of **fresh cilantro leaves**, to garnish

A crunchy raw relish to go with your curry. Or in a sandwich. Or sprinkled over Curry Chips (see page 210). Anywhere you fancy, really.

Tip the shallots into a bowl and sprinkle over a pinch of salt. Toss and let stand for 5–10 minutes—this softens the onions and mellows their flavor. Rinse and drain.

Add the tomatoes and cucumber, squeeze over a little lemon, and then taste—it shouldn't need any more salt. Finish by sprinkling over the cilantro leaves and serve immediately.

═ TIP ═

Drizzle this with mustard oil—easily found in Asian shops—for an extra burst of peppery flavor.

CHAI MASALA

SERVES 2

PREP TIME: 5 MINS • COOK TIME: 10 MINS

WF • GF • V • DF (if substituting milk) **• NF • SoF** (unless using nut or soymilk)

4 **green cardamom pods**

8 **black peppercorns**

4 **cloves**

1 cup **water**

1-inch stick of **cinnamon**

¼ teaspoon **ground ginger**

1 **strongly flavored tea bag**, torn open, or
   1½ teaspoons **strongly flavored loose-leaf tea**

1 cup **whole milk** (or experiment with nondairy milk)

sugar, **honey**, **maple syrup**, or **agave nectar**, to taste

Rebecca's first taste of chai was on a train winding its way through the state of Karnataka, just outside Mumbai. It is served from tea kettles by chai wallahs who move up and down the trains, pouring out little cups of sweetly spiced tea.

If using nondairy milk you will need to experiment—some will separate when boiled, so it may be safer to gently warm it separately and then mix the chai together off the heat.

Place the cardamom pods in a mortar and pestle and bash lightly, then pop out the seeds (discarding the pods). Add the peppercorns and cloves and pummel to a coarse powder.

Place the water in a saucepan and set over a high heat. Add the freshly ground spices, cinnamon stick, ground ginger, and tea leaves. Bring to a boil, then remove from the heat. Stir in the milk, then bring back to a boil again.

Remove from the heat and strain into cups. Sweeten to taste.

≡ **TIP** ≡

Don't use posh or delicate tea for this. Any robust blend will work.

MINT & GINGER FIZZ

SERVES 8–12
PREP TIME: 5 MINS • COOK TIME: 8 MINS
WF • GF • DF • V • Ve • NF • SoF

FOR THE SYRUP:
¾ cup **water**
1½-inch piece of **ginger**, peeled and cut into matchsticks
5 ounces **sugar**

TO SERVE:
ice
mint sprigs
seltzer or **sparkling mineral water**
salt

A refreshing and summery drink.

To make the syrup, pour the water into a saucepan and bring to a gentle boil over a medium heat. Add the ginger and simmer for 1 minute or so, then add the sugar. Stir to dissolve the sugar, then remove from the heat and set aside to cool.

Strain into a sterilized bottle or jar with a lid, to store. The syrup will keep in the fridge for about 1 week.

To serve, pour about 1 tablespoon of the syrup into a tall glass filled with ice. Take a mint sprig and place it on your palm, then clap your hands together, to release the oils. Place into the glass. Top up with fizzy water, add a tiny pinch of salt, stir, and then taste—add more syrup for a sweeter, more peppery drink. Serve immediately.

LASSI

SERVES 1
PREP TIME: 5 MINS
V • WF • GF • DF (if substituting yogurt) **• NF • SoF** (unless using nut or soy yogurt)

½ cup **whole-milk plain yogurt** (can be nondairy)
½ cup **chilled milk** (can be nondairy)
¼ cup **chilled water**

FOR MANGO LASSI:
3 tablespoons **mango purée** or mashed **fresh mango**
½ teaspoon **sugar**, or more, to taste (optional)

FOR SALTED LASSI:
a pinch of **salt**
a pinch of **dry-roasted ground cumin**

FOR SWEET LASSI:
½ teaspoon **sugar**, or more, to taste
a pinch of **saffron threads**
¼ teaspoon **rose water**, or more, to taste

≡ TIP ≡
If you have a strong enough blender, you can swap the water for 4 ice cubes, and blend until smooth and very cold.

This classic, cooling yogurt drink can be made sweet, salty or fruity.

If using mashed fresh mango, then you will need to prepare this in a blender, but all the others can be made using a whisk.

Blend or whisk all the ingredients together, then taste—how much sweetness or other flavorings you add is very much down to personal taste, or to the ripeness of the mango.

BREAD

NAAN

MAKES 8 BREADS
PREP TIME: 20 MINS, PLUS 2 HOURS 20 MINS RISING/PROVING • COOK TIME: 6 MINS PER BREAD
V • Ve • DF (if substituting yogurt and ghee) **• NF • SUITABLE FOR FREEZING**

2 teaspoons **active dried yeast**

1 cup **lukewarm water**

2 teaspoons **sugar**

5 tablespoons **whole-milk plain yogurt** (you can use nondairy yogurt)

3 tablespoons **ghee** (vegan or dairy-based), melted, plus extra for brushing

14 ounces **unbleached bread flour**

4 ounces **all-purpose flour**, plus extra for dusting

1 teaspoon **fine salt**

neutral oil, for oiling bowl

1–2 teaspoons **nigella seeds** (optional)

☰ TIP ☰

To get the soft, chewy naans you'll recognize from takeouts, cool (or even freeze) the breads, then mist lightly with water and microwave for 30–40 seconds before serving.

Pillowy, slightly charred breads, served warm and brushed with ghee.

Mix the yeast, water, and sugar together in a bowl and leave for 10 minutes or so for the yeast to wake up; the liquid will become frothy. Stir in the yogurt and ghee, whisking until smooth.

In a large bowl, mix together the flours and salt. Pour in the yeast mixture and mix with a spoon until a rough dough forms. Use your hands to help bring the dough together into a soft, sticky ball. Flour a clean work surface, and knead the dough for 4–5 minutes (or use a mixer fitted with a dough hook). When it is smooth, stretchy, and pliable, tip the dough into a clean oiled bowl, cover with a damp dish towel or plastic wrap, and leave somewhere warm to rise until doubled in size, 1–2 hours.

Turn out the dough onto the floured surface, and use a sharp knife to cut in half, then divide again and again until you have 8 equal pieces. Shape into neat balls, and place on a baking sheet to prove for 20 minutes or so, covered in a dish towel or loosely with plastic wrap.

When ready to cook, set the oven to a low (warming) heat, and set a large (ideally heavy cast-iron) skillet over the highest heat. Let the pan get really hot while you roll out the dough.

Place a dough ball on the floured surface, and flour your hands and a rolling pin. Squash the ball flat with your hands, squishing and patting it out into a circle. Pick up the dough, and let gravity stretch it into an oval, turning the dough by 180° so it becomes longer. When it is about 8 inches long, place it on the surface and roll out to ¼ inch thick and about 9 x 10 inches. Don't worry if this seems thin—it will puff up during cooking.

═ VARIATIONS ═

FOR GARLIC NAAN: Blanch 1 clove of **garlic** in boiling water for 3 minutes, then crush and mix with melted **ghee** and chopped **cilantro**. Brush the mixture over the cooked naan.

FOR CHEESE NAAN: Shred 4 ounces of **mozzarella** and mix with **salt**, **pepper**, crushed **garlic**, chopped **shallot** or **scallion,** and **crushed red pepper**. Sprinkle over a layer of cheese after rolling out the dough, then fold and gently roll it out again. Cook as here.

FOR PESHWARI NAAN: Mix 5 tablespoons each of **ground almonds** and **desiccated coconut** with 2 tablespoons **golden raisins** (optional), 4 tablespoons melted **ghee** or **butter**, or more if needed, and 2 teaspoons **superfine sugar**, until it forms a thick paste. Squash a dough ball flat, then place a generous tablespoon of filling into the center before folding the edges in, to form a ball again. Gently roll out and cook as here. Beware: They'll be extremely hot on the inside, **as they will puff up and fill with scalding steam.**

Dust off excess flour from the dough, then carefully place in the hot, dry skillet. Cook for about 2 minutes, until the bottom of the dough is freckled with brown spots and bubbles have appeared on top, then flip. Do this again once or twice, until the bubbles are just beginning to scorch, but don't allow the bread to burn.

Remove from the pan and brush lightly with melted ghee, then sprinkle over a pinch of nigella seeds, if using. Keep warm, wrapped in a dish towel in a low oven, until all the breads are cooked.

ROTI & CHAPATI

SERVES 4 (MAKES 8 BREADS)
PREP TIME: 15 MINS • COOK TIME: 3 MINS PER BREAD
DF • V • Ve • NF • SoF • SUITABLE FOR FREEZING

10 ounces **chapati/atta flour** (or 50:50 **whole-wheat** and **all-purpose flour**), plus extra for dusting

1/3 teaspoon **fine salt**

about ¾ cup **water**

2 teaspoons **neutral cooking oil**

Roti and chapati are very similar flatbreads and go with almost any Indian-style curry. Since they are unleavened, they take almost no time to make.

In a large bowl, stir together the flour and salt. Add enough of the water to form a dough (it shouldn't be sticky, so you may not need it all) and the oil. Bring together with your hands and, when it forms a rough ball, tip it onto a clean, floured work surface. Knead for 4–5 minutes, until the dough feels smooth and springy (or use a mixer fitted with a dough hook). Don't skimp on the time needed for this step—you need to stretch out the gluten or the finished breads will be tough.

Divide the dough into 8 equal pieces and shape into neat balls. Flour a rolling pin and the surface again and roll each ball into an 8-inch disc, about ¼ inch thick.

Place a large skillet over a medium-high heat. When hot, place the first bread in the dry pan. Cook for about 1 minute, or until little bubbles appear on the base of the bread. Flip, then repeat twice more, cooking for about 30 seconds each time, until no raw patches remain and a few little bubbles have charred but the bread is still soft and floppy.

Wrap the bread in a clean dish towel and keep warm while you cook the rest. Use a sheet of paper towel to carefully wipe away any charred flour collecting in the pan.

Serve the breads warm, to scoop up saucy curries or dhal.

≡ TIP ≡

To make your roti puff up, once cooked, place each one in the flame of a gas stove for 10 seconds (but be careful they don't burn).

METHI THEPLA

MAKES 8 BREADS
PREP TIME: 20 MINS • COOK TIME: 5 MINS PER BREAD
DF • V • Ve (if substituting yogurt) • **NF • SoF** (unless using nut or soy yogurt) • **SUITABLE FOR FREEZING**

7 ounces **chapati/atta flour** or **whole-wheat flour**

2 ounces **all-purpose flour**, plus extra for dusting

1 ounce **chickpea flour/besan** (or substitute **all-purpose flour**)

½ teaspoon **ground turmeric**

½ teaspoon **ground coriander**

¼ teaspoon **asafetida** (optional)

½ teaspoon **fine salt**

4 tablespoons **whole-milk plain yogurt** (or **nondairy yogurt**)

up to ½ cup **water**

2 ounces **fresh** or **frozen fenugreek leaves** (not dried) (defrosted and excess water squeezed out, if frozen), finely chopped, tough stalks discarded

½ teaspoon **peeled and grated ginger**

1 teaspoon **neutral cooking oil**, plus extra for frying

≡ TIP ≡

Many recipes for methi thepla include finely chopped green chili pepper, crushed red pepper or chili powder, or cilantro leaves, so feel free to experiment.

These delicious flatbreads are made with chopped fenugreek leaves (methi), which we buy in frozen blocks, like spinach, in the supermarket, but you can also get them fresh in Asian food stores.

In a large bowl, stir together the flours, turmeric, coriander, asafetida, if using, and salt. Add the yogurt and about half the water and mix. As a rough dough starts to form, add the chopped fenugreek leaves, ginger, oil, and just enough water to bring everything together—the leaves will release water as they are kneaded, so keep the dough as dry as you can.

Turn the dough onto a clean floured surface and knead for 4–5 minutes, until it feels smooth and elastic. Roll into a log shape, divide into 8 equal pieces, and shape each piece into a neat ball. Using a floured rolling pin, roll each ball into an 8-inch disc, about ¼ inch thick.

Place a large skillet over a high heat. Use a heat-resistant brush or spatula to lightly coat the pan with oil, then slide in the first bread. Cook for about 2 minutes, until speckled with golden bubbles on the bottom. Brush the top of the bread with oil and flip. Cook for another 2 minutes until golden bubbles appear on that side, too. If any raw-looking spots remain, flip once or twice more.

Wrap the breads in a clean dish towel and keep warm while you cook the rest. Serve immediately.

RINKU'S SPICY WATER BOMBS (PUCHKAS)

MAKES 30
PREP TIME: 20 MINS • COOK TIME: 10 MINS
DF • V • Ve • NF • SoF

30 **ready-made pani puri puffs** (you can buy these online or in Indian food stores)

FOR THE FILLING:
3 medium **waxy potatoes**, peeled and cut into very small cubes
14 ounces **canned black chickpeas (kala chana)**
1 **red onion**, very finely chopped
1 **green chili pepper** (or more, to increase the heat level), finely chopped
3 teaspoons **chaat masala spice blend**
1 teaspoon **salt**
2 tablespoons **finely chopped fresh cilantro**
1 tablespoon **rapeseed oil**

FOR THE TAMARIND WATER
5 tablespoons **Tamarind Chutney** (see page 217, or use store-bought)
½ teaspoon **chili powder**
½ teaspoon **ground cumin**
lemon juice or **tamarind paste/concentrate**, as needed (optional)

Rinku is one of Rebecca's friends and she served these puchkas at a party thrown by Rebecca and Steve (photographer for this book) when they opened their own studio last year. "This incredible pop-in-the-mouth snack can be found on every street corner in Kolkata. People even compete to devour the most in the shortest time. This version comes from my parents, who have used it to entertain loved ones for decades. For our street food stall, Raastawala, we renamed them Spicy Water Bombs because of the explosion of flavors."

To make the filling, place the cubed potatoes in a saucepan and cover with water. Bring to a boil and simmer for 10 minutes, until tender. Drain immediately and set aside to cool.

Mix the remaining ingredients for the filling together in a bowl. When the potatoes are cool, add and mix together.

To make the tamarind water, mix everything together with ½ cup water to form a loose sauce. Taste—it should be quite tangy. Add a squeeze of lemon juice or a teaspoon of tamarind paste or concentrate, if needed.

To assemble: Just before serving (to avoid soggy puchkas), take each pani puri puff and gently knock a hole in the middle of one side with the back of a teaspoon. Repeat with all the puffs. Spoon 1 teaspoon of filling into each puff.

To eat, pour about 2 teaspoons of tamarind water into the filled puff and immediately pop into the mouth. Or simply serve with the water alongside.

PARATHA

5 ounces **chapati/atta flour**

2 ounces **all-purpose flour**, plus extra for dusting

½ teaspoon **salt**

6 tablespoons **ghee**, melted

about ½ cup **water**

These flaky Indian flatbreads are a real treat. The way they are coiled and rolled out before cooking gives the dough rich, buttery layers.

Place the flours in a bowl, add the salt and 2 tablespoons of the ghee, and use your hands to rub the fat in, until it feels sandy. Add enough water to make a dough, adding it little by little so it doesn't become sticky. Shape into a ball and knead for a full 5 minutes (or use a mixer fitted with a dough hook). Wrap in plastic wrap or a clean, damp dish towel, and let rest for 30 minutes.

With the remaining melted ghee nearby, divide the dough into 8 small balls (or 4–6 larger balls). Dust a work surface and rolling pin with flour, and roll out each ball to a thin 9-inch disc. Sprinkle with flour, then use a pastry brush to lightly brush the tops with melted ghee. Tightly roll up the discs into sausage shapes, then coil into spirals. Tuck the outside ends underneath the spirals.

Place in the fridge for 15 minutes to firm up (or in the freezer for 5 minutes).

Remove the coils from the fridge and dust everything with flour again. Squash each coil flat with the palm of your hand, then roll out to 8-inch discs. Stack the discs with parchment paper between each one to stop them sticking.

When ready to cook, set a large dry skillet over a medium heat. When hot, brush the top of one of the breads with melted ghee and place in the pan, ghee-side down. After about 2 minutes, when bubbles appear on the top, brush that side with ghee, and flip. Cook until beginning to brown, then flip again. Flip once or twice more, until the bread is golden brown all over. Set aside and keep warm while you cook the rest. Serve immediately.

═ TIP ═

Ghee is an Indian cooking fat made from butter, although there are vegan versions available in large supermarkets. It's easy to find, but if you can't, use unsalted butter or even cooking oil instead, making sure to wipe out the pan after cooking each bread, as leftover butter will burn. Chapati flour is easy to find in Asian food stores and online—if not, use a 50:50 mixture of whole-wheat flour and all-purpose flour.

RINKU'S PEA-STUFFED PARATHA

MAKES 15 FLATBREADS

PREP TIME: 30 MINS, PLUS 30 MINS RESTING TIME • COOK TIME: 10 MINS, PLUS 6 MINS PER BREAD

DF • V • Ve • NF • SoF

FOR THE DOUGH:

1 pound **chapati/atta flour**

1 pound **all-purpose flour**, plus extra for dusting

¼ teaspoon **salt**

1 teaspoon **rapeseed oil**

FOR THE FILLING:

1 pound **frozen peas**, defrosted

1½-inch piece of **ginger**, peeled and finely grated

½ **red** or **green chili pepper**, finely chopped (optional)

½ teaspoon **salt**

1 tablespoon **rapeseed oil**

1 teaspoon **cumin seeds**

2 teaspoons **asafetida**

These delicious flatbreads are Rinku's mother-in-law's recipe, and a family favorite. They are easy to cook and great to make with kids.

To make the dough, place the flours and salt in a bowl and mix well. Add the oil and a tablespoon of lukewarm water. Mix and add water a dash at a time, to form a soft dough and no flour remains on your hands. Tip out onto a floured surface and knead for 4–5 minutes (or use a mixer fitted with a dough hook). Cover with a damp dish towel and let rest for 30 minutes.

To make the filling, place the peas, ginger, chili pepper, if using, and salt in a food processor. Blitz briefly, until combined but still coarse, with plenty of chunks of pea left. Heat the oil in a skillet over a medium heat. Add the cumin seeds and cook just until fragrant, taking care not to burn them. Add the pea mixture and stir-fry gently for 5 minutes. Stir in the asafetida and cook until the mixture begins to look dry and a little crumbly, about 5–10 minutes. Remove from the heat and let cool.

Shape the dough into 15 equal balls. Flatten one with both palms into a disc, then press your thumb against the edges, to make thinner and larger. Hold the disc in your cupped palm and fill with 2 teaspoons of pea filling. Bring the sides of the dough into the center and pinch the edges to seal. Repeat for all 15 portions, then gently roll each ball out on a floured surface to about 8 inches in diameter, taking care not to roll so hard that the filling breaks through.

Place a skillet over a medium heat. When hot, cook a paratha for 2–3 minutes, or until it begins to change color and a few brown spots appear on the bottom. Flip, brush the top with ¼ teaspoon oil, cook this side, and repeat. Remove from the pan, wrap in foil, and keep warm while you cook the rest. Serve immediately.

≡ TIP ≡

This is a great way to surreptitiously get an extra green vegetable into the tummies of small children.

RINKU'S EGG KATI ROLL

MAKES 4

PREP TIME: 15 MINS • COOK TIME: 5 MINS PER KATI ROLL

V • NF • SoF (check paratha ingredients)

½ **cucumber**, cut into thin julienne slices

1 **onion**, finely sliced

2 **red chili peppers**, deseeded and finely chopped

1 tablespoon **freshly squeezed lime juice** (about ½ lime)

4 **eggs**

salt

2 tablespoons **neutral cooking oil** (optional)

4 **parathas** or **other flatbreads** (homemade, see pages 205–206 or 198–201, or ready-made), uncooked

½ teaspoon **black salt** (optional)

lime wedges, to serve

Raastawaala—Rinku's street food stall—is famous for selling kati rolls. "For every Bengali from Kolkata, this egg kati roll holds a special place. Traditionally bought by workers on their way home as a filler until their next meal, now tourists from all over the world make a point to try (and re-try) one. You can use lots of other fillings. Almost any leftover Indian-style curry will work: try chana masala, keema, sag paneer or chicken tikka masala, as well as raita."

Place the cucumber, onion, and chili peppers in a bowl. Squeeze over half the lime juice and mix, then set aside to allow the ingredients to pickle lightly. In another bowl, crack one of the eggs and whisk it with a pinch of salt.

Place a medium skillet over a medium heat. When hot, and if using homemade paratha, add 1½ teaspoons of oil. (If you're using ready-made paratha, you can probably cook directly in a dry, nonstick pan.) Place a paratha into the hot pan and cook until golden spots begin to appear on the underside. Flip and cook the other side until it starts to turn golden, then use tongs to lift the bread from the pan.

Pour the beaten egg into the pan, spreading it out quickly to the size of the paratha, then place the partly cooked paratha directly on top. Press down gently, to ensure that both the bread and the egg cook fully, about 1 minute. Remove and keep warm while you cook the rest in the same way.

To assemble: place a sheet of parchment paper on a plate and then a paratha, egg side up. Sprinkle with a pinch of black salt, if using. Add a row of pickled salad, followed by a squeeze of lime juice. Roll up, using the parchment paper to enclose the roll and twisting the sheet at the end. Repeat for all the parathas and serve.

TIP

In Kolkata, tomato ketchup is often served with kati rolls, to use as a dip or drizzle. Parathas are quite rich, so you can substitute rotis or chapatis, if desired.

CURRY WRAPS & CURRY FRIES

. . . .

Leftover curry is a real treat—and is often better than when freshly made.

. . . .

CURRY FRIES

. . . .

SERVES 4
PREP TIME: 20–30 MINS • COOK TIME: 20 MINS
Can be WF • GF • DF • V • Ve • NF • SoF

. . . .

1 pound **frozen fries**

8 heaped serving spoons **leftover saucy curry**—Chana Masala (page 94) is particularly good, but any will work

TO SERVE:

Raita (page 163 or 164)

one or all of the following chutneys:

Mango Chutney (page 216), **Lime Pickle** (page 214), or **Cilantro Chutney** (page 215)

Indian-style salad—we love the pickled onions from Rinku's Egg Kati Rolls (page 209) or Kachumber Salad (page 192)

fresh cilantro

finely sliced **red chili peppers**

Who says curry has to be with rice? We've been serving baked fries at LEON since 2012—they go with everything.

. . . .

Cook the fries according to the directions on the package.

Meanwhile, reheat the curry until piping hot.

Serve the fries topped with the curry, garnished generously with chutney(s), raita, Indian salads, cilantro leaves, and chili peppers. Devour. Ideally with beer.

CURRY WRAPS

SERVES 4

PREP TIME: 15 MINS • COOK TIME: 5–10 MINS

Can be **DF • V • Ve • NF • SoF**

leftover Indian-style curry, of your choice

one of the following spiced proteins:

leftover Onion Bhaji (page 154);

leftover Spiced Lamb Chops (page 101), meat stripped and roughly chopped;

leftover Curry-Spiced Tofu (page 102);

leftover Lamb Keema (page 145)

4 large **flatbreads/wraps**

4–6 sprigs of **tender mint**

a handful of **fresh cilantro**

4 tablespoons **pomegranate seeds**

½ **red onion**, finely sliced

4-inch piece of **cucumber**, sliced into long thin pieces

Raita (page 163 or 164), for drizzling

one or two, or all, of the following chutneys (store-bought or homemade):

Mango Chutney (page 216); **Cilantro Chutney** (page 215); **Tamarind Chutney** (page 217); **Lime Pickle** (page 214)

finely chopped **red chili peppers**

4 **crisp lettuce leaves** (romaine or little gem lettuces work well)

To make a good wrap, you need a mixture of firm, chunky (not saucy) curry or spiced protein, crunchy veg and sauce.

Thoroughly reheat whichever curry and/or protein you have chosen to use.

Warm the flatbreads/wraps, either in a low oven or directly over a gas flame for 30 seconds (do this as needed, for each wrap as you make them).

Lay a bread out flat in front of you (if you want to prevent leaks, lay a sheet of foil or parchment paper underneath to wrap everything in at the end). Spoon one-quarter of the curry in a vertical line in the middle of the bread, starting about one-third from the bottom. Place any protein in a line next to it. Top with the herbs, pomegranate seeds, and a few slices of onion and cucumber. Drizzle over some raita and any chutneys, then finish with a sprinkle of chili peppers and a lettuce leaf.

Fold up the bottom section of the wrap (which shouldn't have any fillings on it) to enclose about half the fillings. Fold in each side of the wrap, tightly enclosing the fillings like an envelope. If you used paper or foil, use it to wrap everything further. Repeat with the other breads. Eat immediately.

PICKLES & CHUTNEYS

LIME PICKLE

MAKES 6–10 PORTIONS
PREP TIME: 15 MINS, PLUS UP TO 4 WEEKS PICKLING • COOK TIME: 1 MIN
WF • GF • DF • V • Ve • NF • SoF

10 **limes**, stems removed, washed throroughly

6 tablespoons **freshly squeezed lime juice** (about 3 limes)

1 teaspoon **ground turmeric**

4 cloves of **garlic**, crushed

1-inch piece of **ginger**, peeled and finely grated

2½ tablespoons **fine salt**

2 tablespoons **sugar**

¼ teaspoon **asafetida**

1½ teaspoons **chili powder** (or more, to taste)

1 tablespoon **paprika**

FOR THE TEMPER:

6 tablespoons **neutral cooking oil**

1 tablespoon **black mustard seeds**

½ teaspoon **fenugreek seeds**

1 teaspoon **nigella seeds**

a pinch of **cumin seeds**

1 teaspoon **fennel seeds**

6 **curry leaves**, roughly torn

Is there anything better than a dollop of hot and sharp lime pickle next to a portion of curry or loaded onto a shard of pappadam? Yep... If it's pickle you've made yourself.

Slice each lime into 4 wedges (or 6 if large), then cut each segment into 6–8 small pieces, widthways. Place in a bowl with the remaining ingredients (except the temper) and mix well.

To make the temper, heat the oil in a small saucepan over a medium heat. When hot, add the mustard seeds and, when they begin to pop, add the fenugreek, nigella, cumin and fennel seeds, and let sizzle for 30–50 seconds. Remove from the heat, add the curry leaves, and sizzle briefly, stirring. Tip the tempered spices into the bowl with the lime. Mix well, then taste for heat levels—if you love really hot pickles, you may want to add some more chili powder, or even crumbled dried chili peppers.

Pour everything into a large sterilized jar with a lid (1-quart capacity, or use 2 or 3 small jars), allowing a 1-inch gap at the top. Leave for 2–4 weeks (the longer the better), turning the jar upside down every couple of days. Once opened, store in the fridge for around 1 month. Use clean spoons when serving or the chutney may go moldy.

≡ TIP ≡

Open carefully, in the sink or wearing an apron, as the jars will release little splashes of spicy oil.

CILANTRO CHUTNEY

This hot, sweet, sharp emerald-green chutney contains no artificial preservatives, so it's best to make it in small quantities and eat it quickly. We serve it alongside Indian vegetable curries, with dhal and yogurt, in our favorite Curry Wraps (see page 211), or even slathered into a Mumbai-style sandwich. Try adding peanuts, crushed garlic, chopped chives or shallot, or even a dollop of yogurt.

a handful of **fresh cilantro leaves**, stalks removed, washed well, and very finely chopped

¾-inch piece of **ginger**, peeled and grated

1 tablespoon **freshly squeezed lemon juice**

¼ teaspoon **ground cumin**

2 generous pinches of **asafetida** (optional)

2 tablespoons **oil** (**vegetable**, **sunflower**, **olive**, or **rapeseed**)

1 teaspoon **sugar**

½–1 small **green chili pepper**, deseeded and finely chopped, to taste

¼ teaspoon **chili powder** (optional)

¼–½ teaspoon **fine salt**

Place all the ingredients except the chili powder, and using only ¼ teaspoon salt to start with, into a mortar and pestle or into a tall container to fit an immersion blender. Pound or blitz very well, until about as smooth as pesto. Taste and decide if you want to add the rest of the salt or the chili powder, or even more sugar or lemon. It should be tangy, sharp, a little salty, and a little sweet, with a good level of heat from the chili pepper.

Store in a lidded container in the fridge, for no more than 2 days. A layer of foil or plastic wrap pressed over the top will help prevent the cilantro from discoloring.

MANGO CHUTNEY

MAKES 2 X 14-OUNCE JARS
PREP TIME: 20 MINS • COOK TIME: 1 HOUR
WF • GF • DF • V • Ve • NF • SoF

a pinch of **cumin seeds**

a pinch of **coriander seeds**

4 **green cardamom pods**

¾ cup **white wine vinegar** or **apple cider vinegar**

8 ounces **sugar**

1½ teaspoons **fine salt**

1½-inch piece of **ginger**, peeled and finely grated

1 clove of **garlic**, crushed

a pinch of **nigella seeds**

½ teaspoon **paprika**

2 ripe **mangoes**

Fruuuuuuuity. And not too sweet.

In a hot dry skillet, toast the cumin seeds, coriander seeds, and cardamom pods for 1 minute or so, until just fragrant. Tip into a mortar and pestle and bruise lightly. Set aside.

Place the vinegar, sugar, salt, ginger, and garlic in a deep nonreactive saucepan and bring to a simmer, stirring until the sugar dissolves. Add the bruised spices, along with the nigella seeds and paprika. Reduce the heat and simmer while you prepare the mangoes.

If the mangoes are very ripe, work over a large bowl to catch all the lovely juices. Using a small sharp knife, cut a line around the middle of the mango, then do the same lengthways. Peel off one-quarter of the skin and cut chunks of the flesh away from the pit. Repeat with the next quarter and, when the pit is revealed, trim away as much flesh as you can. Repeat until all 4 quarters have been cut away from the pit. Cut the flesh into ¼-inch pieces.

Add the fruit and any collected juices to the pan and bring back to a boil. Cook for 50–60 minutes over a medium heat, carefully stirring often so the bottom doesn't burn, until reduced by about half and nicely thickened.

While piping hot, carefully pour into clean sterilized jars and immediately cover with lids. It will keep for months, sealed. After opening, store in the fridge and use within 2–3 weeks.

COCONUT CHUTNEY

SERVES 4 AS A RELISH
PREP TIME: 8 MINS • COOK TIME: 3 MINS
WF • GF • DF • V • Ve • NF • SoF

Delicious with everything from samosas to bhajis.

1 tablespoon **vegetable oil**

2 teaspoons **mustard seeds**

a generous pinch of **cumin seeds**

1 teaspoon grated **ginger**

8 tablespoons **desiccated coconut**

½ cup **freshly boiled water**, or more as needed

a pinch of **salt**

Heat the oil in a small saucepan over a medium heat. When hot, add the mustard and cumin seeds and toast, just until they begin to crackle. Remove from the heat, stir the ginger into the pan, and let sizzle.

Tip the desiccated coconut into a bowl and add the freshly boiled water, along with the toasted spices and salt. Mix together and add more boiling water until you get a good consistency—it should be thick rather than watery, but not stiff. Leave to cool before serving.

RINKU'S EASY TAMARIND CHUTNEY

MAKES ABOUT ½ CUP
PREP TIME: 5 MINS • COOK TIME: 7 MINS
WF • GF • DF • V • VE • NF • SoF

"This chutney is a sweet, sour, tangy brown sauce. It's super-popular in India and goes with almost anything (I think of it as a ketchup equivalent). Drizzle it on savory dishes, or serve as a dip. Traditionally, it is made with dried tamarind, which is boiled and reduced for hours—this is my easy version."

1½ teaspoons **cumin seeds**

5 tablespoons **tamarind paste** (choose a good-quality paste with no fibrous strands)

3 tablespoons **jaggery** or any **dark brown sugar**

1 teaspoon **chili powder**

½ teaspoon **salt**

4 tablespoons **water**

Dry-roast the cumin seeds in a skillet over a medium heat, just until fragrant. Grind to a powder in a mortar and pestle.

Place the ground cumin and all the other ingredients into a saucepan, mix well, and bring to a boil. Reduce the heat and simmer for about 5 minutes, until the chutney thickens. Remove from the heat and let cool.

When cool, place into a clean sterilized jar and seal. The chutney can be refrigerated for up to 2 weeks.

INDEX

A

aloo tikki 158
Asian greens: steamed greens 180
  Thai-style fried rice 175
  see also bok choy
asparagus: chicken meatball coconut
  curry 71

B

balti: Emily's amazing Birmingham balti
  149–51
beans *see* black beans; green beans;
  kidney beans
beef: beef Madras 53
  beef rendang 131
  Cape Malay curried beef 34
  massaman curry 22
  Shumaiya's akhni pilau 177
beets: beet and coconut
  curry 63
  beet thoran 184
  Rinku's beet pachadi 167
Bengali fish tenga 29
bhajis: onion bhajis 154
bhuna: fish bhuna 113
Birmingham balti 149–51
biryani: chicken biryani 146–8
black beans: Caribbean-style black
  bean curry 57
  coconut rice 'n' peas 178
black dhal makhani 135
bok choy: chicken meatball coconut
  curry 71
  steamed greens 180
Bombay potatoes 187
bread: curry wraps 211

methi thepla 201
naan 198–9
paratha 205
Rinku's egg kati roll 209
Rinku's pea-stuffed paratha 206
Rinku's spicy water bombs 202
roti and chapati 200
broccoli: steamed greens 180
  tofu phad phrik khing 97
Burmese-style fish, shrimp, and tomato
  curry 109
butternut squash: butternut, chickpea,
  and kale curry 136
  Erica's lentil masala 72

C

'ca ri ga' Vietnamese chicken curry 21
cabbage, pea, and potato curry 183
cafreal: Chiara's grandmother's Goan
  chicken cafreal 54
Cape Malay curried beef 34
Caribbean chicken and mango curry 30
Caribbean-style black bean curry 57
cauliflower: baked aloo gobi 188
  cauliflower rice 170
  quickest curry ever 98
  Sri Lankan-style jackfruit curry 121
chai masala 193
chana masala 94
chapati 200
cheese: cheese naan 199
  sag paneer 60
chicken: 1960s chicken tikka masala
  16–17
  'ca ri ga' Vietnamese chicken curry 21

Caribbean chicken and mango
  curry 30
Chiara's grandmother's Goan chicken
  cafreal 54
chicken biryani 146–8
chicken chettinad 76
chicken dopiaza 142
chicken meatball coconut curry 71
Colombo de Martinique 33
doro alicha'a tibs 117
Emily's amazing Birmingham balti
  149–51
jungle curry 49
kuku paka with ugali 138–9
Nilgiri curry 67
Shumaiya's family chicken korma 64
Thérèse's chicken katsu and curry
  sauce 25
chickpeas: butternut, chickpea, and
  kale curry 136
  chana masala 94
  Rinku's spicy water bombs 202
  West African-style peanut curry 84
chili peppers 10
chutneys: coconut chutney 217
  cilantro chutney 215
  mango chutney 216
  Rinku's easy tamarind chutney 217
clams: Thai-style clam curry 122
coconut: beet and coconut
  curry 63
  chicken meatball coconut curry 71
  coconut chutney 217
  coconut rice 168

coconut rice 'n' peas 178
coconut sticky cauliflower rice 170
lemongrass coconut eggplant
    curry 80
Sri Lankan-style coconut dhal 79
Colombo de Martinique 33
cilantro: cilantro chutney 215
    Nilgiri curry 67
    Rinku's pomegranate and cilantro
    raita 164
corn: chicken meatball coconut curry 71
    jungle curry 49
cornershop curry 90
cornmeal: kuku paka with ugali 138–9
cucumber: kachumber salad 192
cumin: jeera rice 169
curd rice 168

D
dhal: black dhal makhani 135
    everyday dhal 26
    Sri Lankan-style coconut dhal 79
dhansak: lamb dhansak 132
dopiaza: chicken dopiaza 142
doro alicha'a tibs 117
drinks: chai masala 193
    lassi 195
    mint and ginger fizz 194

E
eggplants: eggplant and tomato
    curry 125
    jungle curry 49
    lemongrass coconut eggplant
    curry 80
eggs: curry udon noodles 14

egg-fried rice with soy sauce 173
    gym bunny curry 114
    Rinku's egg kati roll 209
everyday dhal 26

F
fenugreek leaves: Matt's lamb keema 145
    methi thepla 201
fish and seafood: baked mackerel
    curry 93
    Burmese-style fish, shrimp, and
    tomato curry 109
    cornershop curry 90
    curried shrimp stir-fry 118
    fish bhuna 113
    Lipu's Bengali fish tenga 29
    skinny parcel-baked salmon and
    zucchini curry 89
    South Indian-style fish curry 83
    Thai fishcakes 157
    Thai-style clam curry 122
fries: curry fries 210

G
gap year curry 44–6
garlic naan 199
ghee 205
ginger: mint and ginger fizz 194
Goan chicken cafreal 54
goat: heartbreak curry 38–9
green beans: chicken meatball coconut
    curry 71
    cornershop curry 90
jungle curry 49
    quickest curry ever 98
    Sri Lankan-style green bean and

zucchini curry 106
    Sri Lankan-style jackfruit curry 121
    steamed greens 180
    tofu phad phrik khing 97
green curry 44–6
greens 11
    baked mackerel curry 93
    kuku paka with ugali 138–9
    steamed greens 180
    tofu phad phrik khing 97
    see also Asian greens; broccoli; chard;
    kale; spinach
gungo peas: coconut rice 'n' peas 178
gym bunny curry 114

H
heartbreak curry 38–9

I
Indian-style cauliflower rice 170
Indian-style fried rice 174
Indian-style steamed greens 180

J
jackfruit 11
    Sri Lankan-style jackfruit curry 121
jalfrezi: vegetable jalfrezi 98
Japanese-style cauliflower rice 170
jeera rice 169
jungle curry 49

K
kachumber salad 192
kale: butternut, chickpea, and kale
    curry 136
    West African-style peanut curry 84
katsu: Thérèse's chicken katsu and curry
    sauce 25

keema: Matt's lamb keema 145
khao soi gai 75
kidney beans: black dhal makhani 135
    coconut rice 'n' peas 178
    rajma 110
korma: Shumaiya's family chicken
    korma 64
koshambari salad 191
kuku paka with ugali 138–9

L lamb: heartbreak curry 38–9
    lamb dhansak 132
    lamb pasanda 68
    lamb rogan josh 128
    Matt's lamb keema 145
    Shumaiya's akhni pilau 177
    smoky curry-spiced lamb chops 101
lassi 195
lemongrass coconut eggplant curry 80
lentils: black dhal makhani 135
    Erica's lentil masala 72
    everyday dhal 26
    koshambari salad 191
    lamb dhansak 132
    Sri Lankan-style coconut dhal 79
lime pickle 214

M mackerel: baked mackerel curry 93
    cornershop curry 90
Madras curry: beef Madras 53
mangoes: Caribbean chicken and
    mango curry 30
    mango chutney 216
    mango lassi 195

massaman curry 22
meatballs: chicken meatball coconut
    curry 71
methi: Matt's lamb keema 145
    methi thepla 201
mint: mint and ginger fizz 194
    Nilgiri curry 67
mozzarella: cheese naan 199
mung/moong dal: koshambari salad 191
mushrooms: curry udon noodles 14
mutton: heartbreak curry 38–9

N naan 198–9
Nilgiri curry 67
noodles: crunchy deep-fried noodles 74
    curry udon noodles 14
    khao soi gai 75

O onions: chicken dopiaza 142
    crispy onions 179
    onion bhajis 154
    see also shallots

P pachadi: Rinku's beet pachadi 167
pakora see bhajis
paneer 11
    sag paneer 60
paratha 205
    Rinku's egg kati roll 209
    Rinku's pea-stuffed paratha 206
parcel-baked salmon and zucchini
    curry 89
pasanda: lamb pasanda 68
peanut butter: West African-style

peanut curry 84
peas: cabbage, pea, and potato curry 183
    Matt's lamb keema 145
    pea and potato samosas 161–2
    Rinku's pea-stuffed paratha 206
    steamed greens 180
peppers: quickest curry ever 98
peshwari naan 199
pickles: lime pickle 214
pilau: Shumaiya's akhni pilau 177
polenta: kuku paka with ugali 138–9
pomegranate and cilantro raita 164
pork: pork vindaloo 50
    Thai red curry with crispy pork
    belly 43
potatoes: aloo tikki 158
    baked aloo gobi 188
    baked mackerel curry 93
    Bombay potatoes 187
    cabbage, pea, and potato curry 183
    curry fries 210
    massaman curry 22
    pea and potato samosas 161–2
    Rinku's spicy water bombs 202
puchkas 202

Q quickest curry ever 98

R raita 163
    Rinku's pomegranate and cilantro
    raita 164
rajma 110
red curry with crispy pork belly 43
rendang: beef rendang 131

rice: basic steamed white rice 9
   black rice 169
   cauliflower rice 170
   chicken biryani 146–8
   coconut rice 168
   coconut rice 'n' peas 178
   curd rice 168
   egg-fried rice with soy sauce 173
   Indian-style fried rice 174
   jeera rice 169
   Shumaiya's akhni pilau 177
   Thai-style fried rice 175
rogan josh: lamb rogan josh 128
roti 200

S

sag paneer 60
salmon: Burmese-style fish, shrimp, and
   tomato curry 109
   skinny parcel-baked salmon and
      zucchini curry 89
salted lassi 195
samosas: pea and potato samosas 161–2
seafood see fish and seafood
seitan 11
shallots: kachumber salad 192
shrimp: Burmese-style fish, shrimp, and
   tomato curry 109
   curried shrimp stir-fry 118
South Indian-style fish curry 83
soy sauce: egg-fried rice with soy
   sauce 173
spices 10
   see also individual spices
spinach: baked mackerel curry 93

sag paneer 60
snowpeas: steamed greens 180
split peas see yellow split peas
Sri Lankan-style coconut dhal 79
Sri Lankan-style green bean and
   zucchini curry 106
Sri Lankan-style jackfruit curry 121
sugar snap peas: steamed greens 180
sweet potatoes: West African-style
   peanut curry 84

T

tamarind: Rinku's easy tamarind
   chutney 217
   Rinku's spicy water bombs 202
   tamarind yogurt 165
tea: chai masala 193
tenga: Lipu's Bengali fish tenga 29
Thai fishcakes 157
Thai food 47
Thai red curry with crispy pork belly 43
Thai-spiced tofu 105
Thai-style cauliflower rice 170
Thai-style clam curry 122
Thai-style fried rice 175
Thai-style steamed greens 180
thoran: beet thoran 184
tikka masala: 1960s chicken tikka
   masala 16–17
tofu 11
   curry udon noodles 14
   curry-spiced tofu 102
   Thai-spiced tofu 105
   tofu phad phrik khing 97
tomatoes: eggplant and tomato curry 125

baked mackerel curry 93
Burmese-style fish, shrimp, and
   tomato curry 109
kachumber salad 192

U
udon noodles: curry udon noodles 14
ugali: kuku paka with ugali 138–9

V
vegetables 11
   vegetable Jalfrezi 98
   see also individual vegetables
Vietnamese chicken curry 21
Vietnamese-style steamed greens 180
vindaloo: pork vindaloo 50

W
West African-style peanut curry 84
wraps: curry wraps 211

Y
yellow split peas: everyday dhal 26
   lamb dhansak 132
yogurt: curd rice 168
   lassi 195
   raita 163
   Rinku's beet pachadi 167

Z
zucchini: skinny parcel-baked salmon
   and zucchini curry 89
   South Indian-style fish curry 83
   Sri Lankan-style green bean and
      zucchini curry 106

ABOUT THE AUTHORS

REBECCA SEAL has written about food and drink for the *Financial Times*, the *Evening Standard*, the *Observer*, the *Guardian*, *Red* and *The Sunday Times*. Her cookbooks include *Istanbul: Recipes from the Heart of Turkey* and *Lisbon: Recipes from the heart of Portugal*, as well as co-authoring *LEON Happy Soups*, *LEON Happy One-pot Cooking* and *LEON Fast Vegan* with John Vincent. She is one of the food and drink experts on Channel 4's *Sunday Brunch*. She lives in London with her husband and two small daughters.

JOHN VINCENT is Co-founder of LEON, which now has more than 60 restaurants (including in Amsterdam, Utrecht, Oslo and Washington, DC). He wrote *LEON Naturally Fast Food* with Henry Dimbleby, *LEON Family & Friends* with Kay Plunkett-Hogge, *LEON Happy Salads* and *LEON Fast & Free* with Jane Baxter and *LEON Happy Soups*, *LEON Happy One-pot Cooking* and *LEON Fast Vegan* with Rebecca Seal. He thinks that our relationship with food should be positive and joyous and that we need to listen more carefully to our gut, eat more good fats and less sugar.

ACKNOWLEDGMENTS

JOHN

Rebecca is the most wonderful partner in the kitchen. As is Katie, my partner in all the other rooms. Thank you both.

REBECCA

What a joy this book was to create. If you like food and someone suggests that you might like to work on a compilation of the best curries from around the world, you jump at the chance—I think that was true for everyone who worked on this project. First, thank you to John Vincent, for once again giving me the chance to be part of the lovely LEON family and to write this with him. Thanks also to Rebecca Di Mambro, Ottie Ise and Charlotte Baly, along with everyone at LEON who helped put this together.

The book's fabulous good looks are down to photographer Steven Joyce, food stylist Sian Henley and props stylist Lauren Law, and we couldn't have done it without the assistance of Tom Groves and Charlie Crosley-Thorne, who always go beyond the call of duty to make our shoots work perfectly. Thank you to the brilliant design team at Octopus Books for pulling it all together, as well as our Publisher Alison Starling, along with Creative Director Jonathan Christie and editors Pauline Bache and Sophie Elletson, who make it all make sense.

We love being able to include recipes from our friends, and friends of LEON, and we are so grateful to Davide Ghetaceu from Ethiopian Flavours, Shumi Khan, Emily Hawkley, Thérèse Gaughan, Chiara Pinto and Erica Molyneaux for letting us include their wonderful dishes. I owe particular thanks to my friend Rinku Dutt, who gave us more recipes than anyone else and taught me a lot about curries along the way, too.

I also owe a debt of gratitude to the food writers who have inspired me over the years, and knowingly or unknowingly, their past recipes have helped us write this book: Diana Henry, Maunika Gowardan, Meera Sodha and Madhur Jaffrey in particular. I feel seriously lucky that this is my job.

An Hachette UK Company www.hachette.co.uk

First published in Great Britain in 2019 by Conran Octopus,
an imprint of Octopus Publishing Group Ltd
Carmelite House, 50 Victoria Embankment
London EC4Y 0DZ
www.octopusbooks.co.uk

Distributed in the US by Hachette Book Group
1290 Avenue of the Americas,
4th and 5th Floors, New York, NY 10104

Distributed in Canada by Canadian Manda Group
664 Annette St., Toronto, Ontario, Canada M6S 2C8

Text copyright © LEON Restaurants 2019
Design and layout copyright © Octopus Publishing Group 2019

Recipe on page 54–5 © Chiara Pinto; recipes on pages 28–9, 64–5 and
176–7 © Shumaiya Khan; recipe on page 72–3 © Erica Molyneaux; recipe
on page 116–17 © Davide Ghetaceu; recipe on page 144–5 © Matt Sefton;
recipe on page 149–51 © Emily Hawkley; recipes on pages 164, 166–7,
202–3, 206–7, 208–9 and 217 © Rinku Dutt

ISBN 978-1-84091-797-0
Printed and bound in China
10 9 8 7 6 5 4 3 2 1

Photography by Steven Joyce

Publisher: Alison Starling
Creative director: Jonathan Christie
Senior editors: Pauline Bache and Sophie Elletson
Copyeditor: Emily Preece-Morrison
Food styling: Sian Henley
Prop styling: Lauren Law
Designer: Ella Mclean
Senior production manager: Allison Gonsalves

We have endeavored to be as accurate as possible in all the preparation
and cooking times listed in the recipes in this book. However, they are an
estimate based on our own timings during recipe testing, and should be
taken as a guide only, not as the literal truth.

Nutrition advice is not absolute. If you feel you require consultation
with a nutritionist, consult your GP for a recommendation.

Standard level spoon measurements are used in all recipes.
1 tablespoon = one 15ml spoon
1 teaspoon = one 5ml spoon

Eggs should be large unless otherwise stated and preferably free range
and organic. The Department of Health advises that eggs should not
be consumed raw. This book contains dishes made with raw or lightly
cooked eggs. It is prudent for more vulnerable people such as pregnant
and nursing mothers, invalids, the elderly, babies and young children to
avoid uncooked or lightly cooked dishes made with eggs. Once prepared
these dishes should be kept refrigerated and used promptly.

Fresh herbs should be used unless otherwise stated. If unavailable, use
dried herbs as an alternative but halve the quantities stated.

Ovens should be preheated to the specific temperature—if using a
fan-assisted oven, follow manufacturer's instructions for adjusting the
time and the temperature.

This book includes dishes made with nuts and nut derivatives. It is
advisable for customers with known allergic reactions to nuts and nut
derivatives and those who may be potentially vulnerable to these aller-
gies, such as pregnant and nursing mothers, invalids, the elderly, babies,
and children, to avoid dishes made with nuts and nut oils. It is also
prudent to check the labels of pre-prepared ingredients for the possible
inclusion of nut derivatives.

Vegetarians should look for the 'V' symbol on a cheese to ensure it is
made with vegetarian rennet.
Not all soy sauce is gluten-free—we use tamari (a gluten-free type of soy
sauce), but check the label if you are unsure.

Remember to check the labels on ingredients to make sure they
don't have hidden refined sugars. Even savory goods can be artificially
sweetened so it's always best to check the label carefully.